Applause

"So compelling is Catherine's writing. If I merely put my eyes upon it, it captures my chaotic mind and takes me into (and amuses me greatly) the reveries of her past. There is the comfort of the similarity in all our family stories, and then, there is her unique take on those stories—years of therapeutic delving gives a wonderful, accepting and objective look at the human condition. Bottom line: it is a FUN read and highly recommended!"
—PJ Tyler, Astrologer, Cardinal Star Systems

"Catherine, I can't always find the words to convey how deeply felt many of your stories are to me. They enrich my spirit and validate me that somehow other things I have read do not."
—Linda Troolin

"Your writing is funny, compassionate, and very, very honest—a rare and wonderful combination."
—Alison Tinsley, co-author of *Meditation: If You're Doing It, You're Doing It Right.*

"Catherine, cheering for you and your brave, honest, funny and tender stories that bless us by showing the cracks in our hearts."
—Carole Peccorini, blogger, *Conversations That Matter*

"Love what you write, how your write, why you write, and for sharing it, my friend."
—Bob Rice

Catherine Sevenau

QUEEN BEE

Reflections on Life
and Other Rude Awakenings

Tintype Publishing
Sonoma, California

Tintype Publishing
P.O. Box 1206, Sonoma, CA 95476
Sevenau.com
CSevenau@earthlink.net

Editor, content development and line editing:
Deb Carlen, Five-Ideas.com

Book midwife, final edit, cover and interior layout design:
Ruth Schwartz, TheWonderlady.com

Content organization, editing, and midnight advice:
Cory Gilman

Cover art:
Sarah Niebank, Mandala Healing, digital artist
fineartamerica.com/profiles/sarah-hoffman.html

Cover image:
License granted by ©National Portrait Gallery, London, England
Queen Elizabeth I, NPG 5175
npg.org.uk/collections/search/portrait/mw02070/Queen-Elizabeth-I

Author photo:
In Her Image Photography
InHerImagePhoto.com

QUEEN BEE: Reflections on Life and Other Rude Awakenings
Catherine Sevenau —1st edition.
ISBN-13: 978-0-9960514-2-2   (paperback edition)
ISBN-13: 978-0-9960514-3-9   (eBook editions)
Library of Congress Control Number: 2015921278

Dedicated to My Teachers

Stephanie Moore
Through her I found not only grace, I found my voice.

Michael Naumer
Before working with Michael, I was asleep.
After working with him, so the song goes,
"I can see clearly now..."

*What can I write about today? I could write about what rises
from the ashes, I can write about what we don't understand.
Or I can write about gratitude.*

—Stephanie Moore (1951 – 2006)

*Sometimes you eat the bear,
and sometimes the bear eats you.*

—Michael Naumer (1942 – 2001)

Last night as I was sleeping, I dreamt—marvelous error!—
that I had a beehive here inside my heart.
And the golden bees were making white combs and
sweet honey from my old failures.

—Antonio Machado (1875 – 1939)

Table of Contents

ROOTS

PUTTING PEN TO PAPER

HY WRITE? IT'S COMPLICATED. I never had any intention of becoming a writer, to externalize my life and expose it on paper. Then, as life would have it, I had a meltdown as the result of a course I was in, and from that meltdown I wrote a short piece called "Queen Bee," the first story in this book. That's how all this started nearly fourteen years ago.

Writing fulfills a need to celebrate those I love, and those who have loved me. It is a way I can be seen and heard, to have something useful to say and the courage to say it. I can get on a royal tear about things, and yes, I can be vaingloriously all about me, but it provides me with an opportunity to better understand myself and to present myself on behalf of something larger than me. It allows me to ask the questions I consider worth asking, and perhaps, to answer them. I write to smuggle the stories from my mind into yours. Writing allows me to clarify my thoughts and ideas, to explore the things I'm afraid of. Every story matters, and if I can find meaning for myself, perhaps I can help others find it. Isn't that the main task of a storyteller? My writing reflects the best parts of me and it gives shape to my life. It's good for my soul. It is also the only way to get my mind to pipe down.

I write about my mother. I put in black and white what I know, or think I know. I write about possibilities and perspective. Incidents that crack me up or make me weep spill onto paper. I do wax poetic, but my lines rhyme, which I hear is out of style. I write about what matters to me, about sin and prayer, hope and gratitude, about where I beg to be healed.

1

I write about those I love and those who irritate me, even when they're one and the same. I chronicle stories of fools, friends, and family, including the dead ones. I've spent years disturbing the dead in my family, digging up their stories and studying their photographs. The last section of this book is for them. I believe I'll heal my soul by rounding up all of us and telling our tales. I write to leave their legacy, and mine.

Queen Bee: Reflections on Life and Other Rude Awakenings is a compilation of short pieces I've composed over the years. Some are from my blog, many I've posted on Facebook, others are recently written. Most are stories I have felt called to write. A few are in memory of those who passed. There is a chattering of exchanges with my young grandchildren, mostly snippets, while others are chunks of longer conversations.

The pieces herein I've written over the years. Some are dated, others I can't remember when I wrote them. Some also include redundancies, written at various times for different audiences. Bear with me, it's how I roll.

I invite you to careen around with me in the back seat of my mind. It's always lovely to have company. We can hold hands across the pages and share tears in between. We can snort and hoot and holler. And hopefully, by the end, we'll tell one another it was a great trip. Life, even with its continual barrage of rude awakenings, is always a ride.

—*Catherine*

REFLECTIONS

QUEEN BEE

I AM THE QUEEN BEE. You know how I know? My friends tell me, and I also have a pair of blue bikini panties with a queen bee on them that proves it. I have been known as the Carrot Juice Queen, the Dance Floor Queen, and the Queen of Curb, Gutter and Sidewalk. I don't like to show country property; for one thing, it wrecks my high-heeled shoes, and for another, there might be things out there that could get me. I am Her Highness in my family, Her Oneness in class, and Her Eminence at my work.

I am the Queen of Complaint and the Queen of Control. And why not? This world would be a much better place if everyone would just do it the right way. Besides, if I didn't try to control everything, well, who would? It might just all fall apart. I am clear it is up to me to be in charge. It's the Queen's job!

I am the Queen of Funny. Every once in a while, though, I hang out with my sons—just to make sure I don't get *too* queenly. You see, my sons don't think I'm so funny. I just think I have what you might call a "timing problem" with them. I gave my younger son a cartoon and in it this therapist is slapping his patient upside the head telling him to, "Snap out of it!" The caption in the corner reads, "SINGLE SESSION THERAPY."

"I suppose," he said, "you think that's funny." I thought it was hilarious. Apparently he didn't. He takes after his father.

I am also the Queen of Confusion. I know right from left because I salute the flag with my right hand. But in dance class my teacher would say, "Now come forward on your right foot" and I'd do that and my partner would lean into me, and whisper politely, "Your other right foot." I do know up from down, however. Look, there are plenty of gas stations out there if ever I need more directions than that.

Last week I went to see a healer as my bones have been aching so much. He told me, "Your bones are fine—it's your mother. She hasn't passed over yet, and she needs your help to get to the other side." *They must not have any gas stations where she is.* I'm 53 now—the same age she was when she killed herself 33 years ago. He said she was my spirit guide, said I had a lot of work to do soon and would need her help, and said she couldn't help me until her journey was complete. He told me to put food and water for her on my altar every day, to pray for her and for my ancestors before I went to sleep at night. "I'd be willing to do that," I said, and thought, *"I'll place some there for Michael too, just in case he's still wandering around."*

As a kid, I knew I wasn't a queen. I was invisible and it didn't seem to matter if I was there or not; sometimes I'd sneak a look in the mirror to see if I really existed. I thought something must have been wrong with me, and if I could be perfect, well, I might be able to fix what was wrong. It's been a big job, and I'm awfully tired.

But I've been making up for all that these last few years— and what I know in my regal heart is that everything is perfect, and that surrendering is my work. I've wired it up for almost fifty years to protect this Queen of Hearts and it's taking some time to undo these bindings, piece by piece. I have to be careful as I think my heart might be cracked as it hurts so much sometimes. I have help, too. I have honeybees in my heart, making honey from my fear, shame, resentment, and guilt.

I now know I have the heart of a queen, filled with courage and love. You know how I know? My friends tell me. And sometimes—when I take a peek in the mirror—I can see it too.

March 2002

HEARTS TRUMP
EVERYTHING

I LEARNED A LOT FROM PLAYING CARDS, more than just shuffling, cutting, and dealing—like how to win, and how to lose. I realized that pouting didn't improve my hand one whit. I got the hang of the rules, how to keep score, and how to count. I learned how to bluff. I mastered keeping my cards close to my chest, and when to hold 'em and when to fold 'em. I learned to lead with my strong suits, and to play my bad cards as well as I could. I got that cheating wasn't fair, or all that much fun. I learned to play the cards dealt me even when they were rotten, and that it was only a game and not to take it too seriously. I learned about the Ace of Hearts and the Queen of Spades, and that hearts trump everything and hope trumps anything. And I learned that there was always a new hand soon to be dealt, and possibly, a better one.

Unleashing the Flying Monkeys

WRITING A MEMOIR IS ONE THING, having others read it is another; it's akin to being a nude model for the first time in front of an art class. But standing naked in front of strangers (or worse yet, in front of family, friends, and everyone in town) has nothing to do with me or what I look like—it's simply being willing to be seen. So far, no one has smote me down for what I've written—though my sister did threaten to put a hex on me before she died.

Journaling about my childhood and family was an act of love. Turning it into a book, an act of faith. Reworking it into a tale that was coherent, an act of perseverance. Publishing it is either an act of trust, or an act of hubris. It's not an autobiography. It's snippets and sketches and vignettes, strung along a timeline well before I came along up until I'm the age of twenty, kneaded into tales from complicated and sometimes messy lives. It's a story that transformed the holes in me that came out of the chaos and heartache into a kind of wholeness, and out of that wholeness, a kind of holiness emerged.

When the full version of *Behind These Doors* is birthed (I took a sidebar and recorded and published twenty stories from it), it may create some changes in my life. I'll probably write a second half as Andy, my book monger, said, "You can't end the book where you do. People like a story where the hero/heroine rises above their circumstances and wins, and you win. They'll want to know how you did that." My dilemma is, how do I handle writing these stories when many of them involve those I love, or was married to, or do business with, or dated? It's not like the people in my life don't hand me an endless stream of material, but it is risky business unleashing the flying monkeys. Last week my son Jon said, "You can write whatever you want about me," and I thought, "*Really?*" I got a call the next day and he'd reconsidered, that perhaps there were some things he'd rather not see in print. Yeah, like that... so I've yet to work out how to write the second part.

The experiences from my childhood shaped me; they gave me the work I needed to do to wake up, took me to the places where I had to stumble to find my gold. I've spent most of my adulthood overcompensating for my young wounds, which is my way of healing them. My ego makes sure I get seen and heard (though at times in inelegant ways). I know it matters that I'm here, and I do make a difference. If I hadn't been so tweaked into feeling invisible and not cared about by my mother, I imagine I wouldn't be so driven. It's been over 45 years since she's been gone, yet she continues to show up in my life like a bad Hallmark card, popping up whenever I'm sideways about something. My original title of *Behind These Doors* was, *If It's Not One Thing... It's Your Mother*, but someone else with mother issues beat me to it.

A combination of choices, karma, and synchronicity delivered me to my doorstep today. I don't have to know how I got here—though a lot of that got sorted out in the process of writing *Behind These Doors*—I simply know this is where I am now. When I pay attention, hang on, and stay on the path on which I'm pulled (a complete act of trust on my part, as I have no sense of direction), I end up where I'm meant to be. Generally it takes me a while to get there, and I often don't like what it looks like. Sometimes I'm anxious, and other times fearless; at times I'm in a snit, then I'm over the moon.

There are times life is hilarious, and then, there are times it just isn't very funny.

So that's pretty much how my life shakes out—and really, isn't that what it's all about—that, and the *Hokey Pokey*?

IT'S ALL ABOUT ME

Life... IT's ALL ABOUT ME—me, and what I want. No one wants to admit that. Why? Because we don't want anyone to think we're self-centered.

Yet, we abhor others who are egocentric, pompous, selfish, highfalutin, inconsiderate, conceited, thankless, vainglorious, ungrateful, egotistical, or self-serving. But if I spot those things in others, the things I hate about other people, the behaviors that irritate me, all those ways that I don't want to show up, then I know I've got those things in me. Not only do I have them in me, but I keep them hidden because I don't want to be seen that way. People might not like me. Acting like that won't make me look good. Being that way is not nice. It's a slippery slope. It's slightly less slippery when I recognize my dark side, my shadows; then I can dance with them a bit.

Some go: "I'm not all about me, I'm all about you," or "I'm all about this," or "I'm all about that." Right. The only stars in the news these days that are not all about themselves, as far as I can tell, are Pope Francis and the Dalai Lama. They're a tad more evolved than most, in my opinion, and goodness knows I've got plenty of opinions.

I'm perfectly clear I'm all about me—a little tweaked about it actually, probably because I had a mother who was not all about me. She wasn't even sort of about me. The irony of it, though, was that her narcissism and self-centeredness had nothing to do with me; her relationship with me wasn't about me at all—not me, or my value. My timing was bad and she was simply done having children by the time I came along, though as far as I can tell, my siblings didn't fare well with her either. She was struggling to keep her own life together and I played a minor role in her movie—more like a walk-on part actually.

But enough about me. The stories I write are about all of us; we are bound by our humanity and we all have "stuff." People like my writing (some have even told me, so it must be true) because they get another slant on this crazy thing called life or they see something about themselves, about their own upbringing and families. The reflections are not so much about me, but about "we." However, as all roads lead to home, maybe they are all about me.

FALSE HOPE

November 1968 • La Habra, California

WHEN MY MOTHER DIED, her life was packed in a small 1954 two-door, light blue white-topped Hillman Minx convertible. The front seat held her clothes, small feather pillow, and jewelry; the back seat: her black and gold Singer, button collection, and sewing box. In the trunk were her pots, pans, and meat grinder, and her mother's round deco mirror. Tucked in next to her box of family pictures was her blue Samsonite overnight case filled with bottles of pills that through the years kept watch over her like toy plastic soldiers with white caps, standing sentry on her dresser top. She carried a pharmacy with her: diet, pain, and sleeping pills, as well as pills for her stomach, her anxiety and depression and for everything else in the world that ailed her. Over the years Mom lived on green tea, rare steak, and pills: Benzedrine and Dexedrine. Nembutal, Tuinal and Seconal. Librium and Valium. Darvon. Thorazine and Stelazine. There were over-the-counters: aspirin, Excedrin, and a large, cobalt blue bottle of Bromo-Seltzer. My mother, the cosmic omnivore and pharmaceutical zombie.

The five of us spread Mom's possessions on Carleen's living room rug. Larry chose her silver charm bracelet and costume jewelry. Carleen took her sewing scissors and white half-slip. Betty picked the sewing machine, the round mirror, the Dutch oven, the cast iron pans, and the meat grinder. Claudia ended up with her full-length white evening coat and a handful of jewelry. I wanted her Liberty Head necklace and her delicate Gruen wristwatch with the black band. We split up Mom's family pictures, and then we flushed thousands of white pills and colored capsules down the toilet and unceremoniously tossed the stack of receipts that accompanied them. Her button collection and clothes we gave to the Salvation Army. Nobody remembers what we did with her small blue Hillman, though for months it sat in the driveway in La Habra along with the long abandoned Mercury, keeping it company.

There was no funeral, no flowers or friends; only her children came to witness her ashes being ensconced in a cemetery in Brea, and that was only because our brother made us. Mother is now secured behind a small bronze door at the top of a mausoleum wall, high enough where she can no longer get me. Standing there, the five of us were filled with a mixture of relief, regret, remorse, and resentment; we said goodbye and left—and except for my brother Larry—never went back. It didn't matter any more. I thought none of it mattered any more.

If you'd asked me, I would have said I'd given up years ago of her ever wanting me, of listening to or seeing me. But secretly I'd always harbored hope that my mother loved me, my false hope better than no hope at all.

Private Matters

MY FATHER WAS GERMAN and my mother English, which could explain everything. On my dad's side I'm a generation removed from hardworking, church-going, duty-bound dairy farmers. On my mother's I come from freewheeling, drinking, smoking, gambling, hell-raising cattle ranchers with a couple of righteous Catholics thrown in for some temperance. I happen to know my maternal relatives had more fun; I can tell from their stories. Most of them didn't see much value in being good except my Grandma Nellie Chatfield, who was of the opinion that rectitude was required behavior, and the higher she stood on her moral ground, the lower her family descended. I tend to take after Nellie and my father's side of the family. How unfortunate for me, and for those around me, especially those who tend not to behave.

I imagine it's no coincidence that my writing began when I was 53, the same age my mother was when she called it a day. Or that it took me five years to write our chronicles, the same amount of time I lived with her when I was a kid. I have a suspicion she's had a hand in this whole thing, directing from the ethers, enjoying having her story told. She would have LOVED all the attention. My father, on the other hand, would have cautioned me to keep much of what I wrote behind closed doors. He was a private man, of the generation that didn't discuss affairs of the family, money, or sex.

Dredging up some of these stories was a cross between *Groundhog Day* and post-traumatic stress syndrome. It's amazing how long the shelf life is on the defining moments that smack us as kids. They're like Wonder Bread—always fresh.

I made it through my childhood, then I lived through five years of writing about it, which was at times as anxiety-producing as experiencing some of it the first time around. My right shoulder froze, then my left, my stomach wasn't happy, nor was my sister, and I had three computer crashes. In the last one I lost my motherboard. Now what are the odds of that? I didn't even know a computer had a motherboard.

My mother is still with me; I'm continually bowled over how I manage to recreate her in so many of my relationships. The bane of my existence and my greatest teacher, she is a gift that keeps on giving.

My Mother and Me: From A to Z

O VER THE PAST FEW YEARS my mother has been following me around, showing up in my stomach, my bones, and my dreams. She used to be a dull ache inside me, but not so much anymore. Mom wasn't cruel or abusive—there was no sliver to take out, no bullet to remove, no thorn to pluck. In the five years I lived with her, I wasn't raised by co-mission, I was raised by omission, by neglect—but neglect doesn't leave a scar, it leaves a hole. Some say holes are harder to heal.

I've spent the last thirty years trying to fill this hole: with sex and recreational drugs (God bless the 70s!), with work, with dancing, and now with writing. Much like my mother, I've been looking for answers. She went the conventional way of the 1950s, going to doctors up and down the state trying to find out what was wrong with her, getting prescriptions for her angst, depression, weight, sleep, and for whatever else possessed her.

I've gone from A to Z in search of understanding, attempting to heal the ache in my stomach, release the pain in my shoulders and jaw, and let go of the resentment I hold in my body.

I've tried:
- Acupressure and acupuncture. Both helped. So has an Ayurvedic diet. Astrology, however, mystifies me—too

much like math. I'm a Leo with my moon rising and my sun setting, or something like that.

- I've done bodywork, breath work, and Bloomwork. I've had biofeedback, taken Bach remedies, and brought a black Buddha back from Bali.

- I've been to chiropractors. I've had my chart done and my chakras cleansed. I have a crystal on my altar. I'm still on page eight of *A Course in Miracles*.

- I've done dream work, dance work, and death work. I've seen the Dalai Lama.

- I've studied the Enneagram. I missed est, and thought people who did workshops like that were whacked. Of course, that's when I was into working and survival, when the only important thing in my life was keeping a roof over my kids' heads. And though I know it could help, I find exercising boring and painful.

- I've read some Freud, Frankl, and Fernando Flores. I've had my house Feng Shui'd. I've taken folic acid and flax seed, and once owned a fresh carrot juice company.

- I've studied Gurdjeiff. I've done group therapy. No gurus abide in my repository, however.

- I've practiced Holotropic Breathwork, seen holistic doctors, and tried homeopathy. I did the Hoffman Process, which is grueling if you've had the mishap of having several parents.

- I've learned to trust my intuition, I have an understanding of my incident, and I try not to be *too* attached to my identity.

- Jung interests me.

- So do Krishnamurti, karma, and kinesiology.

- I've taken LSD.

- Meditation has helped; I have a mantra. I have Michael's mandala on my wall. I have studied mythology and the muses. I've tried magnet therapy and muscle testing. But I'm disappointed to say, I've had no mystical experiences. Perhaps lightning will have to strike me. That could be my final step, like shock treatments. I don't know though; they didn't do my mother much good.

- Regarding numbers: I'm a type *one* on the Enneagram and a *two* in numerology (this is the extent of my math skills). I'm not interested in non-violent communication—I'd have to quit swearing.

- I've met Oscar Ichazo and I've read Ouspensky.

- I've played with a pendulum. I believe there is planetary consciousness. I've prayed to my ancestors, received psychic readings, and done past life work. The teacher said I'd probably be better off not going there, that my plate was plenty full with my present life work.

- I've tried Qigong—too slow.

- I've read Rumi, Rilke, and Ram Dass. I spent a month at Rio Caliente. I tried reflexology. There are, however, two things I won't do: Rolfing or a ropes course. I lasted two minutes in the first and two hours in the second; both are simply ruses to off you.

- I've talked to my spirit guides and asked for their help. I've shadow danced and slow danced. And I know that surrendering is part of my work.

- I've taken Touch of Sun tinctures. I took an introductory Tantra session and within two minutes my jaw locked up; I

23

knew my father would've never approved. I had a teacher, Michael, who died. He taught me about trialectics, among many, many other things. I miss him.

- I read parts of the Upanishads. Unfortunately no flashes of illumination presented themselves.

- I'm vaguely vegetarian. I try to remember to take my vitamins. A vision quest is NOT on my calendar; I hate camping, and am convinced something out there will get me.

- I've done relationship workshops, writing workshops, and women's weekends. I've done a lot of work, and it's made a difference. I know who I am and how I operate. I know that where I stumble is my gold. I know my answers are inside me, not out there somewhere. I know I can ask for help. And my stomach is much better, although my shoulders and jaw are still pretty tight.

- Sadly, xenoglossy, the ability to speak in an unlearned foreign language, is not in my repertoire.

- I've practiced yoga. I've tried to balance my yin and my yang; my yang is still winning.

- I've never mastered Zen. It's a little slow for me. I keep trying to hear the sound of one hand clapping, but there's still too much racket inside my head.

So after this, after all my seeking and searching, hoping for some understanding, I've come full circle back to my mother. "Why" doesn't matter nearly as much as I thought it did. Mom didn't think about the ripples caused by the rocks she cast in the waters. She wasn't out to purposely make my life unhappy or irritating; she didn't have me in mind when she made her choices. It wasn't about me. Somehow I knew that, even as a kid.

I imagine my mother would have preferred that it turn out some other way, to not have stumbled and tripped through her life leaving a batch of broken and chipped china in her path, dancing a mindless waltz in endless circles. Don't you think she would like to have held the hemmed edge of her billowing skirt and elegantly danced? I do. Like her, I too can be a little clumsy, but unlike her, I learned to dance—to twirl and two-step. I love when I float across a shiny wood floor, gliding and swirling and turning like a warm breeze on tiptoe. I never dreamed I could be a dancer.

Many of mother's belongings have recently found their way back to me. Her heavy pinking shears are now in my sewing box. Her black cast-iron griddle cooks my grilled cheese sandwiches. Her delicate gold watch with the narrow black cloth wristband, her Liberty half-dollar necklace from the 1939 San Francisco World's Fair, and her silver charm bracelet crowded with mementos from her life all keep my jewelry company. Her pictures are on my wall and in my photo albums. Her mother Nellie's round English deco mirror hangs in my bedroom, reflecting all three of our images in my face. I also have her metal meat grinder (the one she ran my right index finger through when I was not yet two), stored in an old workman's aluminum lunch pail, way up high on a shelf in my garage where it can't get me. My sisters and brother must have thought these things important to me, that I should have them. They are. I'm pleased when I use or look at or wear them. They remind me of Mother, remind me of some good parts of her. And they remind me of what I missed.

For years I didn't think about her at all. For a while I thought about her more than I needed to. Now, when I think of her, it's easier, and it feels like we can dance.

A DREAM STORY

MANY OF MY DREAMS, the ones I remember, are of me trying to get somewhere, usually on some odd form of transportation, not knowing how to get there, and often with people following me who think I actually know where I'm going. In one I'm riding a horse, leading the way. In another I'm in an English taxi. Then I'm rolling along in a wheelchair, next on a tricycle, another time on a bicycle. In one dream I'm pedaling away in a pedicab with a group tagging along behind.

One night, just prior to falling asleep, I asked my mother, my father, and my teacher Michael (all deceased) to come to me in my dreams. I recorded the vivid succession of images in a journal as soon as I awoke (October 22, 2002). My dream started with Michael, who'd been gone five months. That part was short, and the only thing I remember was asking him if there was something he wanted to tell me, or if there was anything I needed to know. I tried to listen to what he had to say, but my attention kept wandering, so I don't know if he answered, or if I didn't hear him if he did. The images shifted to my mother, who'd taken her life some three decades before.

I'm at the San Francisco side of the Golden Gate Bridge just past the tollbooth in the slow lane, weaving in and out of traffic, lying face down on an old wooden go-cart that looks like a kid's snow sled with wheels, moving along quickly, making it go faster with my hands and feet. An attractive, nicely dressed woman with straight shoulder-length blonde hair is walking just behind me, and calls to get my attention. "*What does she want?*" I think. I've traveled a good distance, and have no time to talk; I'm trying to get someplace. I ignore her and she calls out again. I race away, lying prone on my vehicle, my face just inches from the pavement rapidly passing beneath me, and weave my way from the slow lane onto the pedestrian lane. She's still following me.

I lose her. In the next instant I'm in front of the house next to the Sebastiani Winery, which is three blocks from where I live, scooting along behind the bushes in case she's still nearby. When I'm sure the coast is clear, I pick up my go-cart and step carefully down the moss-covered stone steps. The next instant I'm at the market in the plaza, which is another three blocks away. As I wend my way through the bazaar, I notice the fascinating stalls look like many I've visited in the town plazas in Mexico—the papayas, oranges, and onions stacked in perfect pyramids surrounded by buckets of stock, irises, and sunflowers: colorful and fragrant. I find myself standing in front of a corner fruit and flower stand where three friends, Moona, Audrey, and Barbara, are showing and selling their artwork from their booth. These three women are just a few years older than me, about the ages of my three sisters, and were a comfort and inspiration when I first moved to Sonoma. They were involved as parents or teachers in Moon Valley School, a small alternative school run by Charlie Price where I sent my sons in the mid to late 1970s, where I became the bookkeeper, and then ran the school for a few years after they'd all moved on. Audrey, Moona, and Barbara were also single mothers who gave me courage to raise two young boys on my own.

Audrey holds up a piece of her work. "It's beautiful, but I don't have time, I'm looking for this place," I say.

She telepathically knows where I mean, and points. It's just around the corner. Three bungalows, white, clean, and crisp—like little connected beach houses, each with one small window and a screened front door—are to my left. I sense my mother is inside the first one on my right. I see the door is open through the screen. I lean my go-cart against the wall, peer in, and in the far corner I see my mother asleep. She looks to be in her mid-forties and I'm a young teenager, the ages we were the last time we saw one another.

It's bright in there and I'm surprised she doesn't have on her black eye mask. I'm nervous about coming in, as I'm sweaty and covered in dust from the road. The room is small and clean, crowded with a few pieces of furniture and barely any space to walk. She is lying on a single white-sheeted twin bed, and next to her are a round white table and small white upholstered chair. Everything is white, white, white. I'm quiet and tentative, not feeling sure of myself, wanting to see and talk to her, but waiting for her invitation.

She waves me over to her bed. "Come sit next to me."

Taking off my jeans so as not to get her bed dirty, I sit with her. I notice she has tubes everywhere: an IV in her arm, a plastic one up her nose and down her throat, a catheter coming out of her. She's ill and I realize she's dying. While she shifts to make herself comfortable, I look around the room and see six or seven framed photos on a tall oak bookshelf near the door. I'm curious if any of them are of me. I discover they are family pictures and we look happy. We aren't all together, but in photos by ourselves, and a couple with two or three of us posing together. My mother is not in any; I'm in three. One close-up by myself—my first or second grade school picture—only I have on a bonnet with a small brim. I think how sweet I was as a child, how fresh and pretty. A second picture is of Daddy and me. The third, I don't recollect who was in it, but there are several of us. I study them; relieved she has pictures of me. She *did* care about me.

My attention turns to her, and I ask, "Is there anything you'd like to tell me, anything you'd like me to know?" At that instant, I wake up.

The next day (in my everyday waking life) I discover in my mailbox a postcard from Barbara, announcing she is giving tarot readings. Dialing her, I say, "I just got your card and this is so weird... last night I had the most vivid dream that you were in."

"You always want to tell people when you dream of them," she says, "as it's significant when we dream about one another."

"Want to hear it?" When I finish, she tells me, "I'm part of a dream circle that meets once a month, and Connie Kaplan, who facilitates dream circles and has published a book about them, is coming up from Los Angeles to be there. Would you like to go?"

I don't know much about dreams, but believe they can have significance, and as this one was so detailed, I wanted help deciphering what it meant. "Absolutely," I said, "When and where?"

A week later my friend Daphne and I join Barbara and a circle of women, some of whom I've met. When Connie arrives, she sits next to me on the couch. She checks in with everyone, tells a story, and then relates a second one of her avoiding serious injury in a four-car collision on the freeway coming up from Southern California. I'm looking at her profile, and as she says "freeway" and turns her face toward me a little, all the hairs stand up on my arms and the back of my neck.

"You're the blonde in my dream," I interject.

Laughing, she says, "Well, you may have been dreaming me to protect me in the accident. Thank you." Then she tells us a story about angels walking through walls, being given messages from the other side, about her experience with the angels at the time of her father's death—all a little far-fetched for my money. The dream circle begins, along with the passing of the talking stick from woman to woman. I find the process interesting. I'm dying to ask Connie about mine, but I'd been told before the circle began that I may not share, as I'm not a member of the group.

When the evening concludes, Connie and I talk outside where I relay my dream to her. At the end, she asks me a couple of questions, then says, "Many dreams have a pun, and the most interesting part of your dream, to me, is your pun: it is where you take off your jeans."

I don't get her point. She goes on, "In that action, you are changing the genetic patterns in your family." She looks at me quizzically, and then says, "You're the only one doing this kind of work in your family—and you can do that, you know."

In that moment, something inside told me that this woman, whom I'd met in a dream, was telling me the truth.

Sam: A Dog Story

I T WAS THE WORST DAY OF HIS LIFE, and I could hear the despair in his shaky voice. My son Matt called from the emergency animal hospital in Sacramento. It was a freak accident. He and his wife Brooke were on their way to the Sierras for a camping weekend. His dog, Sam, secured by two leashes, was in the back of the pickup.

Pulling alongside them on Highway 80, a woman frantically signaled Matt to pull over. He yanked his silver Dodge pick-up out of the fast lane and slammed to a halt. Sam was dangling from the tailgate, not moving. Both leashes were twisted so tightly her collar was strangling her, her back end and legs a bloody mess, eyes rolled back, her tongue hanging from her slack-jawed mouth. Unable to free her, Matt gave up and cut her loose, certain she was dead. He and Brooke held each other up, screaming into the early morning with Sam lifeless at their feet, traffic moving by in the fast lane in slow motion like a bad movie reel on the wrong speed.

Matt heard a small cough. Dropping to his knees he leaned close to Sam's head and whispered, "Are you alive, girl?"

Sam, Matt's nine-year-old yellow Labrador Retriever, loved to lunge to the side of the pickup and bark at the big trucks rushing by, confident that the ties restraining her would keep her on board. But this time she lunged at the semi behind them and flipped out the back end of the pickup going eighty miles an hour. Still secured to the truck by two leashes, she was half running, half dragged, trapped by her ties.

My son blamed himself, ignoring that little voice as he was packing, nudging him to secure Sam closer to the cab rather than the middle. The decision whether to put her down now weighed on his heart and he wanted to know what I thought. I asked him, "If she makes it, honey, what will her life be like… and, how much is this going to cost you?"

A month went by before I saw her in the hospital. I'd waited. I'm not big on dogs: a few I barely tolerate, the rest I avoid. But my aversion for dogs is not why I waited. I was afraid to see how she looked, and it was pretty bad.

A tiny, thin, blue plastic tube snaked up her left nostril, cotton blankets cushioned her all around, a catheter retreated from her backside, and her disintegrated hind feet were in rubber casts. In a purple haze from pain medication, she cocked her head and thwapped her tail in happy recognition, smiled at me, and invited me into her cubicle. Lying with her on the floor, we talk and cry. Actually, she talks and I cry. She says how nice I look in my dance clothes; that this has certainly put her old hip pain in perspective; and what a shock it was cartwheeling over the tailgate… like bungee jumping and discovering the rope is not tied short enough but you didn't know it until you hit asphalt.

She appreciates all the love and attention she is getting, the visits from everyone, the red felt-tip hearts the staff draws on her casts, the green rubber frog her vet tech gave her that stands sentry at her furry front feet, protecting her day and night. She says she'd prefer to lie on the flowers people bring her, like she does in the backyard at home, but she doesn't want to hurt anyone's feelings.

My head is touching hers, so I can hear her. Stroking her soft ears and the part of her back that is still covered with her yellow fur, my hand avoids the rest of her body, which is completely skinned from the pavement and grafting. She looks like half of an uncooked Thanksgiving turkey. Wiping my nose to keep from making a mess all over her, she takes her top paw and moves my hand back in between hers so she can tenderly hold it, and tells me not to worry. With a single last wag, she drifts into a peaceful pharmaceutical sleep.

Breathing together, in and out, softly and evenly, I quietly talk to her while she sleeps. I tell her how beautiful she is; about how much her family, her neighborhood friends, and everyone at Rugworks misses her. I also tell her how the Collins girls across the street are going to set up a lemonade stand to help with the vet costs. I say small prayers for her, and thank her for teaching me to fall in love with a dog. I notice she has lost a lot of weight and tell her she looks better than ever...well, her front half anyway.

I remind her of all her other close calls with Matt: tumbling end-over-end down treacherous ski slopes, sailing over rocky cliffs, paddling down rushing rivers; and since she made it through those, she can make it through this.

I whisper close to her ear, "there are a couple of things you might want to know. Matt and Brooke brought home a small gray kitten last week, and I know you don't have much patience for kittens. They are also having a baby in a few months. You need to heal so it won't hurt when the baby gets big enough to crawl all over you, and maybe the baby won't irritate you nearly as much as the kitten will. You'll get used to them, perhaps even fall in love with them."

Sam is so far the most experimental case at the Animal Care Center in Rohnert Park, a struggling new hospital and the only one of its kind in California, healing her damaged body with science and love. They work Sam daily on the underwater treadmill to exercise her limbs while keeping her weight off her feet. They massage her. They talk to her and pet her. She has become the hospital's beloved mascot and longest resident.

Her doctor quietly appears and joins me on the floor. Gently rubbing the naked places on Sam's body, Dr. Alexander explains to me how new fur is already growing through the rectangular blocks of skin grafted from Sam's sides to her hips and legs. She points out that the puckered ruby patchwork seams are healing beautifully, how her raw front paw pads are growing back and toughening up just fine. And how Sam is finally well enough to be taken outside where she loves to roll her face on the fresh grass, smell the earth, and feel like a dog again.

I'm touched that Dr. Alexander is sitting on this dark, speckled linoleum floor with me at 8:30 on a Friday night. She has done so much for Sam, like keeping her own yellow Lab on call at the hospital for a week, ready and willing to give blood if Sam needed a transfusion.

Suddenly Sam jerks, her eyes flutter, her nose and mouth rapidly twitch, her front paws race wildly. Startled, I'm afraid she's having a seizure. The doctor laughs and says Sam is dreaming. I'm happy she can run, even if it is just in her dreams.

When Matt asked me on the call from Sacramento, "What would you do if it were you, Mom? Would you spend $25,000 on a dog?"

"On a dog? No," I said. "On Sam? Maybe."

Sam has been home from the hospital for a month. Most of her fur has grown back; her hind feet are in small neoprene booties. She carefully, and very happily, chases her soggy green tennis ball in the backyard, lies in the flowerbeds, and is making friends with the small gray kitten, Mahari.

On her first trip back to the hospital for therapy and bandage changes, she carefully walks through the front door by herself. An entourage of twenty people slowly follow her, one by one, two by two, and then a parade as the Pied Piper gingerly makes her way through the reception room, down the long hallway, and into the big recovery room. Arriving at her former bed she turns around a couple of times, lies down, and smiles. The doctors, nurses, and staff are gathered, cheering and clapping. Matt, eyes also brimming with tears, is grateful.

Sam is twelve years old now. Her feet healed but her rear paws look like they are on backwards. She still loves to camp, has outlived the kitty Mahari—killed by a car—tolerates Shiva, the other cat, and is patient with Satchel, the now two-and-a-half -year-old son of the family. I think Sam feels about kids like I feel about dogs, so I tell her what a good girl she is every time I see her and thank her for being so sweet to my grandson.

2003

The Shape I'm In

I OFTEN DREW A SIMPLE HOUSE as a small girl, and other than stick figures and daisies, they were my only attempts at art. A great illustrator turned a rendition of my childhood drawing into the cover for my first book, *Passages from Behind These Doors*—a red house with a peaked roof, a door, a window, and five flowers, surrounded by a tree, some grass, and a sunny blue sky. I later ran a jagged crack through the upper left so it would not appear to be a children's book. Represented on the cover of that book are five shapes, external symbols of our internal psychic states, along with some other representations that meant something to me. Below is a paper regarding these shapes, which I wrote ten years ago.

Signs of Life: Five Universal Shapes

What are the five universal shapes? There is the circle, symbolizing *wholeness*, the square which equals *stability*, the equidistant cross signifying *relationship*, the triangle indicating *goals and dreams,* and the spiral, which stands for *growth*. These five basic shapes are a part of all cultures, appearing in their art and artifacts. They are a part of our language, living, and dreams. They are also a part of me, appearing in my psyche and my everyday life. I grow and dance with these shapes, and as I grow and change, my dance changes too.

Where am I? (The circle, my current growth process, and my place from which I deliver my gifts.)

I am a circle, in wholeness and unity. I am a soft edge, a smooth rim, a wheel in motion. I am at the core of my very nature, my current growth, and where I bring my gifts. My circle is my essence.

However, there are things outside my circle, things I can't be with—about me, about you, about them. I have anger, victim mentality, and thoughtlessness outside my circle. I have blame, judgment, and retaliation outside my circle. I have resentment outside my circle. I have Bush and Enron and right-wing fundamentalism outside my circle. How do I expand to include them, *and* have them contribute to me? Ahh, now that is a question—and a whole other conversation.

I am a creature of comfort. I'm content when my stomach is full, my body warm, and nothing is poking me. When my comfort is at risk, my alarm bells go off to protect me from the certain death of freezing, starving, or exhaustion, even though I'm simply cold, hungry, and tired. I'm a creature of order. The minute I have everything tidy, a little clutter here and a little clutter there pops up, like gophers in a half-dozen gopher holes. Then I frantically bat them down and put everything back nice and neat; it makes me feel like I have control. I'm a creature of perfection, with an eye for detail and for what's missing. Some think I am nitpicking. However, I like my circles perfect.

They are everywhere: the sun, the moon, the earth, the planets are all circles. They are the doorknobs in my house, the polka dots in my robe, the blueberries in my pancakes. They are in a bowl on my blue tiled counter: fresh oranges and grapefruits and melons. They are in my yard: an umbrella table, a bird fountain, a silver gazing ball. They are gumballs and green peas and red holly. They are a wedding band, a string of pearls, and my grandmother's mirror. Everywhere I look there are centers, dots, orbs, and circles. My lamp bases and candles, my steering wheel and tires, my flower pots and stepping stones and plates and pans and bowls. My pores and moles, my irises and pupils. My compact, lipstick tube, pen point and pencil lead. My CDs, records, and my iMac base. The period at the end of this sentence. Michael's mandala on my bedroom wall, my watch face, my hoop earrings, my quarters and nickels and dimes, my drains, dryer door, tea ball, my God, they're everywhere! I'm spinning in circles, just thinking about them.

Circles are social; they are soft and sensitive. They are harmonious, continuous, and endless. Circles are whole. Holes. Holy. We are born, we live, we die—we come full circle. The acorn grows into an oak and the oak tree reproduces acorns to grow more oaks—they come full circle. Mysticism led to formal logic. Formal logic led to dialectics, and dialectics to trialectics. We are now returning to mystery and mysticism—full circle. It's like the line-of-dance in the clip of a country-western two-step and the lilt of a waltz; the couples pass by where they started—full circle.

Where I think I am. (The square currently has my attention and is where I'm most aware and most comfortable.)
I think I am a square. I think my inherent strengths are responsibility, stability, and the ability to be fully committed where I give my word. I'm known and valued for my integrity. My square is my foundation.

A square is also a box, like the one my sister claims I was born in. What does she know? Just because I'm confused at times, just because it's safer in here than out there, just because I can be gullible does not mean I was born in one. Maybe I choose to be in here. Maybe I like it.

Boxes (squares) keep things in, and they keep things out. They are contained, neat, and orderly. They have sharp edges to protect me and defend me. They are dependable, sensible, and useful. You can stack them, live in, sit on, store in, and tie red bows on them. They come in all sizes, but not so many shapes. A square is a square is a square. There are square acres, square inches, and square yards. There are town squares, quilt squares, and graham cracker squares.

If you lay it flat, you have a mat. If you stand it up you have a wall; overhead, a roof, underneath, a floor; cut in half, a door. If you turn a square on its point, you have a diamond, which come in jacks, queens, and kings. An ace of diamonds is handy, too. Squares are hardworking and committed. It takes a lot of energy to constantly keep four corners from bending, folding, or collapsing out of shape. My perfection-ism and attention to detail serve me well, in spite of making me predictable—very, well, square-like. I'm organized (when I'm not cluttered), tidy, logical, and practical. This is not just where I think I am—this is where I *live*. I live in a box step, a rumba, a Traveling Four Corners, the predictability of an old-fashioned square dance. I like it that way.

What are my strengths? (The cross, which assists my growth and comes to me effortlessly.)

The equidistant cross is my strength, my current nature. It symbolizes equality, and even though I want to be special, I know I'm the same. It brings me back to my center. It is a meeting in the middle. It's a venturing out to the four direc-tions: north, south, east and west. It's balanced. It's equal. It's integrated.

My strengths are my process of integration, my people skills, my ability to develop relationships easily. It is my abil-ity to achieve balance: I know it's out there; I see it every time I swing by. But it's hard to walk a cross. Do you retrace your steps, do you meet in the middle and backtrack, do you go from end to side to end to side? How do you do it right? If you're not careful and decide to cross outside, you could be a fish instead. It's confusing. You get cross-threaded. Then what? Cranky, cross-eyed, at cross-purposes.

Some crosses are more tolerated than others:

Acceptable crosses: crossbars, crossbeams, cross-cultural, cross-references, cross-stitches, crossroads, and crosswalks.

Unacceptable crosses: crossbones (unless you are a poison warning label), cross-purposes, cross coaching (especially in personal growth work), cross talking (unless you are Italian or Greek, then it's a genetic issue), and double-crossing.

My final strengths? I'm versed regarding cemetery crosses, proficient with crossword puzzles, and adept with a cha-cha crossover break.

Where is my growth, my motivation? (The spiral, as it points to past challenges and circumstances that motivates my current process of change.)

What stretches me? That question takes me where I don't want to go—but meeting it—readies me for wholeness. It is the spiral, my shadow, my dark side. It stretches and motivates me. The spiral is sexuality, creativity, flamboyancy, all the places, spaces, and paths that can make me nervous. Dust Devils. Cyclones. Tornadoes. Spirals are like bad carnival rides, bad perms, and bad trips—too scary, too curvy, and too mysterious. They are constant change and constant movement. They are messy, confused, unorganized, especially for a square. Squares (where I think I live) are uncomfortable with too much fun. Too much fun is too spontaneous, too out of control, and leads to too much trouble.

Spirals are like a snake, like a plume of cigarette smoke, like the legs of entwined lovers. Spirals make my head hurt. I spiral down, down, down into the dark night of the soul. I spiral down the rabbit hole. I spiral into my shadow; then I have to go to confession.

When I spiral up, however, I find the sacred labyrinth, the pathways in English gardens, and my own process of growth and evolution. Each new level rises, offering me a fresh perspective, allowing my witness to mature, presenting me with expanding possibilities of development and awareness. I am flexible, resilient. I'm the springs in my bed, the struts in my car, the woven hair on my Buddha. I am ingenious, creative, interesting. I'm a tango, a whirling dervish, and a Sufi dancer in disguise.

What are my goals and dreams and visions? (The triangle, my least preferred shape, identifying processes I have outgrown, resist, judge, or dislike.)
I am triangular. Pointy-headed, opinionated, competitive. Not a broad thinker. I want things done the right way, my way. I'm the boss, the leader, the manager. I want to be in charge—I just don't want to be responsible. I have the ability to coordinate and delegate, though I can be impatient when you don't get to the point.

Triads are threes of this and trios of that: love affairs, chords of tones, a section of Pindaric odes. Triangles are the eyes of jack-o-lanterns, the tail feathers of birds, a patch of pubic hair. It is a pyramid, a musical instrument, and George Washington's hat.

I have achieved my goals for the first half of my life. Successful in business, financially stable, a healthy family life (except for my younger son who doesn't speak to me, but he just wants to be mad, and my ex-husband who I judge because he still isn't the father I think he should be), a balanced physical (except for exercise), emotional (that varies from day to day), intellectual (my inability to figure out how to get from point A to point B has nothing to do with my intellect), and spiritual life (to tell you the truth, I have no idea what my spiritual beliefs are, other than to define them by exclusion). I practice living in the present for about thirty-six and a half seconds each day.

Where am I resisting the honoring of my dreams?
I have temporarily stopped writing my book.

I want to let go of my business, but duty, common sense, an affinity for it, and the acquired appreciation of living indoors, keep me there.

I have the desire to wake up, but I'm not about to allow, by choice, the complete dismantling of my ego. Of course a car wreck or bolt of lightning could take care of that in a flash.

In my family, I would like to see the genetic traits of resentment and anger transformed. However, I see where *I* still want to be mad.

The triangle represents my goals, dreams, and faith. It is the Father, the Son, and the Holy Ghost. It is my subconscious, conscious, and super-conscious. It is a three-legged stool; more stable then a two-legged or a one-legged stool. It is trialectics, an expanded school of logic (Oscar Ichazo) containing three parts:

- Change occurs in leaps at pre-established points in a cycle.

- Everything contains within itself the seed of its apparent opposite.

- Change occurs in accordance with one's attraction to a higher or a lower possibility.

Occasionally I have the presence to remember this logic. Really, I try not to believe everything I think, particularly in knowing that I lie straight-faced to myself. I'm so used to my thoughts and emotions dragging me around town that I just don't want to let go sometimes. It's so comforting, believing I'm right.

What is my triangle dance? It's my favorite, the nightclub two-step: gracefully turning on a three-point turn across a smooth wooden dance floor, continually turning away from and returning to my partner's embrace, being totally free, then reconnected, then free, in still-frame moments of time.

I have respect for my process, for my basic expression of my human nature. I know that timing is everything, and it is a time of stasis for me, a time of rest. I honor this time, these shapes, this work. Sometimes I wonder where I will end up; I don't have to give it much thought as my past experience foretells my future, and it is good. I only have to show up, pay attention, and dance my dance.

2004

I wrote the above paper in November of 2004, while attending the University of Creation Spirituality. In her book, *The Signs of Life*, Angeles Arrien, a teacher, author, and cultural anthologist, developed a Preferential Shapes Test, allowing one to discover one's current worldview, her conclusion being the five shapes, "are indeed external symbols of our internal psychic states. The preference for particular shapes is an announcement of the values and process active at any time for an individual, a group, or a whole society."

A couple of years after writing it, I gave this paper to Angeles at one of her book signings in Sonoma, and some weeks later she sent me a beautiful note saying she loved it and how much she liked my writing. Can I find that note? No, I put it someplace. Sadly, Angeles died in April of this year (2014), a huge loss to her students and community. In gratitude, intention, and affirmation, I thank her for what she taught me.

Cha-Ching

ONEY ISN'T MY ISSUE this time around, not that it's
easy or abundant all the time. I've earned my own
money since I was twelve. I've saved it, spent it,
lost it, found it, stolen, borrowed, gambled, loaned, collected,
stashed, donated, and shared it. I have frittered it away and
hoarded it close. I've been foolish and wise with it, thought-
less and smart. I've even dreamt about it: feeling lucky,
finding a small pile of small change at the curb, or feeling
frustrated, coins just out of my reach at the bottom of a pool.

I have put money to good use for myself and for others.
I've been on welfare and in the top 2% of wage earners in the
United States. I can be annoyingly stingy in small amounts,
surprisingly generous in large. I have been completely broke,
and trusted that somehow what I needed would show up. It's
amazing; it always did, and still does. I'm not attached to it,
and, I appreciate having it. I have given to others when it was
needed, and even when it wasn't. I have earned it and invested
well. I know how much easier it makes life, and I'm grateful
for how it appears in mine.

I have a money incident that clings to me like tar: Bobby
(my brother-in-law's little brother) stole my 1954 plain, the
best coin in my penny collection, which I still have by the
way. I was ten years old. Every time I'd get off the phone after talking about that side of the family with my sister Liz, I'd
tell her to tell that little SOB I wanted my penny back.

I groused about the theft of that penny for more than forty
years, until my friend and business partner Linda bought me

one for my birthday from a client of hers who was an avid coin collector.

Seventy-five cents it cost her. Man, that was a lot of time and energy for me to spend on one penny...

I had a teacher who said, "When you get your limits, you get your maturity," meaning, if you haven't experienced something, gone through it and come up against it, you know it not. I surmise that's why money stuff doesn't dog me so much. Michael also said, "The only thing I know about money is that it's better to have it than not." He had a good point, and, he also had money issues. It's the old *we teach what we need to learn* thing.

I have plenty of other issues to work with that keep me busy, places where I'm not quite so "together"—like my mother and significant-other relationships, for instance.

Soul Musings

OW DO I CARE FOR MY SOUL? By dancing and being whirled so fast that the room spins and I shriek! What else? Cowboy boots, painted toenails, and my faded 501s do too. There are lavender fields, weeping willows, and sweet peas; a ripe pomegranate, a preening peacock, and Sam, my son's dog. An armada of leaf-cutter ants, the peculiar praying mantis, and that bewildering baby-blue tree at Cornerstone on Highway 121 not only all feed my soul, they blow my mind.

What else nourishes me? Silver hoops, a carved Buddha, and blown glass; Mary Oliver, John Steinbeck, and Anne Lindbergh Morrow do too. They all sustain me.

What else? Rim rocks, pines, and breezes; a hot bath, a soft blanket, and a damp kiss. A chocolate-chip cookie and a cup of white tea. Finishing a crossword puzzle, puttering in my herb garden, writing, dreaming.

Rio Caliente, Bali, and Sonoma touch my soul—especially Sonoma, my beloved home for thirty-some years. My happy roots are entwined with this valley's, snaking under Broadway, twisting about the Plaza, creeping and crawling and climbing through the hillside vineyards and valley oaks. I'm so fortunate to live here.

Being with my grandson: pushing him on the swing, cradling him when he cries, touching his tiny fingers. I love smelling the sweetness of his skin, watching him watch a butterfly, listening to him burble and hoot, feeling the pulse of his heart as he sleeps on mine.

I honor my soul by not disturbing it. I don't watch violent movies. The television moved out with my sons, and my old radio is silent. Weary of the headlines, I canceled my *Chronicle* subscription. I no longer get ruled, riled, and raked over by front-page grist and gossip, by the constant barrage of consumerism and advertising, nor by the disturbing behavior of political hacks, corporate shills, and shameful clergy. When important events occur in the world, someone will let me know.

For a long time, work fed my soul, then kidnapped it. A year ago I wrested it back. No longer needing to prove my worth, I relinquished my badge of busyness. I'm no longer the first to arrive and the last to leave. My work and I have come to a friendly truce. Ahhh, to have times when I have nowhere to go and all day to get there.

I respect my soul by listening to my intuition, trusting, and forgiving myself. By honoring, observing, and befriending my troubled waters and disowned parts, even my perfectionism, resentments, and crankiness settle into place. I care for it by not taking sides when I am divided, by patiently waiting 'til I sort myself out.

Having time with my family, being thankful for my sons, even when we are not getting along. Remembering my father, making peace with my mother, thinking about Michael. Falling in love. Attending to the details of my ordinary life. Taking care of myself. Doing less.

I care for my soul by being grateful. Knowing I'm connected and knowing I belong. Knowing my soul is inseparable from the world around me, interdependent with my family, with neighbors, friends, and foes. The world is a much smaller planet, all of us intertwined. How can we care for our own souls if we overlook another's?

And, I'm not all that cosmic. I have the tongue of a fish-wife and the mouth of a sailor, nor do I suffer fools gladly. I still gossip, judge, and nag. There are a few folks that I'd like to shake some sense into. I bear my share of continuing con-sumerism, self-indulgence, and self-centeredness. And finally, I admit that I'm unwilling to share my space with ants or mice; my apologies to them, but a visit to me is risky. They can pay me back upon my death—that is their work. This is mine.

November 2004

IN SEARCH OF FUNNY

T A RECENT TALK AT OUR LOCAL LIBRARY, a woman asked me about humor, and how one learns to be funny. I said I don't think you can learn to be funny. Either you are, or you aren't. I told her I thought humor is often closely related to pain, that it arises as a reaction to suffering—like a coping mechanism—that sometimes it's the only thing that gets us through this crazy life.

One can have a sense of humor and still not be funny; they don't necessarily go hand-in-hand. Someone I know announced at a recent meeting that his New Year's resolution was to be funny. My internal response was, *you'd better bring your lunch because you're going to be here for a while.* The guy is so *not* funny, even on a good day.

I've not met anyone with a normal, happy childhood who's really, really funny. I'm not even sure I've met anyone with a normal happy childhood. If they told me they did, I'd think they were quite lucky, or lying. They're pleasant, they're kind, they have a sense of humor, but they're not inherently funny. From what I've seen, most comics had challenging young lives, were raised under difficult circumstances, or suffered some sort of trauma. I think comedy often erupts from a deeper, darker place, offering healing to a wounded psyche. And, not everyone with a crappy childhood is funny. Some turn out mean, others turn out sick, some become the walking wounded, and more than a few become outright whack jobs. Then they blame everything on their childhoods.

Humor is subjective. I don't get British humor; *Monty Python* doesn't do it for me. I eye roll and yawn at movies that make others bust up, like *Airplane, Dumb and Dumber,* and *Ace Ventura.* I sit through them and think, *really???* Racist and raunchy humor are also not my cup of tea. Corny doesn't work for me either, unless you're really old and remind me of my father.

I get that humor is in the eye of the beholder. I tilt to the dry and the absurd, to irony and satire. I loved *Groundhog Day*, *Blazing Saddles*, and *Harold and Maude.* Jon Stewart, Tina Fey, and Robin Williams crack me up. Bob Newhart cracks me up. I even crack me up, but I'm easy.

I'm funny—not because I'm inherently disturbed, though that may be—but that because if I didn't laugh, I'd cry. When I was a child I'd burst into tears if anyone looked at me cross-eyed. I was crushed by the slightest criticism and cried when my sisters made fun of me. I sobbed through Disney movies, and *Bambi* nearly did me in. The female tongues in my family flick with meanness, and as I was over-sensitive and dorky to begin with, I had to toughen up to survive. I can still be a dork, which oddly enough has generated some of my best stories and most hysterical moments. I don't know what happens; it's like I become possessed or indignant, and then the moment gets hold of me and snowballs downhill from there. Family or friends standing by slither away, pretending as if they've never seen me before. My response (after I've felt bad if I've hurt someone's feelings) is usually, *ah, heck with 'em if they can't take a joke.*

A fine crack within me separates my laughter and pain, my humor and hurt; with time, events on one side of the crack seep over to the other, and with perspective, the ability to filter the pain or hurt through humor makes life bearable.

There are occasions I get hooked, where things happen and I lose *my* sense of humor. I attended an Angeles Arrien lecture in Santa Rosa during a time when my younger son wasn't talking to me. She was speaking about clarity, objectivity, discernment, and humor: all qualities embedded in the archetype of wisdom. I'd done a lot of personal growth work, seen more about myself than I'd ever in a day cared to see, and one thing that still pained me was my relationship with my son—there was not one iota of humor in there. I knew it was bringing to the surface all my mother stuff about being ignored and not cared about. It really didn't have much to do with him, but it still had me by the throat. No matter how I attempted to work it out or tried to let it go, the more entangled I got—like Br'er Rabbit and the Tar Baby. At the end of her talk she took questions from the room. I stood up in front of a couple hundred people and said, "I'm stuck here. I have a son who's not spoken to me for the last three years, and it's killing me. And you know what, I just don't find it very f****ng funny." The whole room cracked up. Angeles looked at me in kindness and said, "Like that. Look, I get it. But until you get some distance from this, some humor, you will stay stuck." Her response settled me some, but it took me a couple more years to get there. Today, Jon and I are on good terms, but I still find it difficult to find the humor from that time.

Despite the chaos, sadness, and anger swirling around in the world, I do think what transpires is generally funny. It's like some large cosmic joke, like, you know, woe! Life is funny like that. Except when it's not. But laughter is basic, not to mention healing; it takes the edge off, lightens your load, improves your mood, and stimulates the immune system. It's a lot like good sex, except you don't catch any diseases.

I only know one joke, about a string that walks into a bar, but I screw it up every time I tell it.

To me, this is funny; I so wish I'd written it:

"With all the sadness and trauma going on in the world at the moment, it is worth reflecting on the death of a very important person, which almost went unnoticed last week. Larry LaPrise, the man who wrote The Hokey Pokey, died peacefully at age 93. The most traumatic part for his family was getting him into the coffin. They put his left leg in... and then the trouble started."

2015

DHARMA

"**W**E'VE BEEN BROUGHT HERE for a very short time, against our will, and we don't know why." I love that line.

What *is* the point of our birth and life and death? Why *are* we here? What *is* our true purpose? These thoughts keep some of us up at night; others have never examined the questions. Some think life is meaningless, that it has no purpose, that it is simply a terrible misunderstanding. Others make it mean whatever they want it to mean.

I don't believe any of us are here on a whim; I think each of us has a purpose—even if only to serve as a warning for the rest of us. But for whatever reason that we are in these bodies on this planet at this time, we all have gifts to give, we all make a difference, and we want to matter.

Suppose that we are here to discover our true selves, and to serve others through our unique, creative expressions. I've been fortunate to have talented teachers in my life—mentors who lived according to their true callings, knew their purposes, their reasons for being. Two are paramount, and both have died. In May of 2001, Michael Naumer, a man whose life's work was about consciousness and transformation, died from lung cancer. Actually, he took his own life to end his unbearable pain. He didn't have much time to live, so he chose to leave early. My dance and writing teacher, Stephanie Moore, died from uterine cancer. She went out in January at the tail end of the wild storms that hit Northern California in late 2005 and early 2006. Stephanie was also not one to go gently into the night.

Both Michael and Stephanie understood their dharma, their true purposes and unique vocations in life. They held their teaching—be it dance, writing, or consciousness—as their responsibility and duty to others, and it's what they lived for. Not everyone could hear what they had to say, or were interested, but many hung on for the ride, and it was wild. They taught us to create and live up to our standards, not theirs, and to see the world with wider eyes. They brought out the best in many of us, turned us into dancers who felt our own rhythms, writers who found our own voices, and questioners who found our own answers. Rattling our cages, they shook loose our cobwebs. They were committed, passionate, on fire, and gave generously of themselves. Death ended their lives, but not my relationships with them. I forever nod to them for rocking my boat.

I met Stephanie when I was 39; over the next five years she taught me to dance, which was no small feat for someone with two left ones. I'd left my body as a child as there were times when it was dangerous to inhabit it. I think, because of that, I'd no sense of space or direction and was constantly tripping, bouncing off doorframes, or knocking things over—a thin, wan, train wreck covered in tattered Band-Aids. Dancing moved me back into my interior. I grin when I am referred to as elegant; if they only knew. I've been twirling and two-stepping for 28 years now, and I bless Stephanie whenever the sound of a waltz drifts my way.

Then my friend changed her direction in life from accomplished dance instructor to gifted writing teacher. At the age of 53, I picked up a pen and wrote a small piece called "Queen Bee" and from that, I found myself for the next few years in Steph's Monday night writing class. That was the genesis of my family memoir.

I met Michael when I was forty-six. In 1995 I took his and his wife Christina's three-day course, the *Mind of Love*, and continued with the graduate work as it morphed into *Beyond the Game*. Michael also gave me the opportunity to assist him in the weekend workshops for the last two and a half years they were offered. All in all, I took that course twelve times, along with five continuous years of Tuesday night graduate classes. I've done so much transformational work, you'd think I'd be enlightened. Michael's work influenced my thinking, writing, and way of being. I began to understand that things were happening *for* me, not *to* me. I developed the ability to turn my index finger around, without breaking it, to see *my* part. I learned that the mind is a dangerous neighborhood, and not to go in there alone.

These two will always be a part of my daily dance. I can still hear Stephanie's coaching: "That was perfect... just one thing." I also hear Michael's echo at the end of many a point: "...and then some."

So why am *I* here? Looking for my life's purpose was like a fish looking for water: though it was all around me, it took me a bit to see it. When I examine my commitments, where I direct my energy, where I lose track of time amidst my total absorption, my unique gifts became apparent: I'm a connector, here to keep "family" together—historically, biographically, and personally. I'm here to be a storyteller, to make people think and to make them laugh. I'm here to teach: I know a lot about some things and a little about others. These engagements, individually and in concert, dance inside my heart.

I didn't choose the ways in which I've spent my life— rather, they subtly chose me. I get this magnetic pull inside me where wild horses couldn't stop me. I didn't *plan* on starting a carrot juice company, any more than I *planned* on owning a real estate business. Nor did I *plan* on getting married and being a mother, a businesswoman, a seeker, a dancer, or a writer. Life happens. My childhood, genetics, and karma have played a part, as have the choices I've made. I listen to that pull in my gut, even when it makes no sense. I pay attention to the clues that come my way, and connect the dots.

I notice when synchronicity appears. Curiosity, trust, and excitement propel me on the path of creating and doing what I love. It's endless and ever changing. I don't worry when I'll get there, as there is no *there*, so I follow my heart and continue on that winding path, wherever it may lead. It also matters not that I have no sense of direction; I always end up where I need to be, even when I'm not happy with where I am.

There was a time when I struggled, when I had no idea what I was supposed to be doing to make a difference. In my angst, a wise friend and teacher gently put his hand on my shoulder and said, "You don't have to *do* anything, you just *be* you." Seems easy enough: to show up and simply be me, except for those times when I want to be right or am annoyingly bossy. Then I get to be the warning for others. Oh, well. Sometimes you get to be the windshield; sometimes you get to be the bug.

2015

A Higher Possibility

ICHAEL AND HIS WIFE Christina distilled concepts from the consciousness movement into courses they created and led over the years. *The Mind of Love*, which morphed into *Beyond the Game*, incorporated principles from Gurdjieff, Oscar Ichazo, Werner Erhard, Ram Dass, and numerous others in the human potential movement. They brought to the forefront conversations on choice, reality, logic, and transformation. The objective of their work was self-recognition, based on the premise that, "The purpose of relationship was not to make oneself happy, but was a useful vehicle for seeing oneself." *Beyond the Game* was a higher game: it was a game of chess, not checkers, and it was a game not to be missed. It was also a game that changed me.

40 Principles, Tools, and Aphorisms from Michael Naumer

1. Consciousness is that which recognizes itself.

2. Everything changes. Everything happens in cycles. Everything contributes.

3. Everything contains within itself the seed of its apparent opposite.

4. Everything is important—and nothing is significant.

5. There are no accidents.

6. Things are not happening *to* me, they are happening *for* me.

7. Do I want to be right, or do I want to be effective?

8. Am I available for what I say I want?

9. What is my part?

10. Expand to include and have it contribute.

11. There is no meaning in reality. Truth does not *mean* anything, it's just *what's so*.

12. No good deed goes unpunished.

13. The mind is a dangerous neighborhood; don't go in there alone.

14. Our baggage is the material we need to transform. We need our stuff, we just want to become objective about it so we can deal with it.

15. If you are going to be there, be there. If not, go someplace else.

16. Whatever you hold as *this shouldn't be*, you energize its continued existence.

17. What you can't choose, you have to hold as burden.

18. Where you are the most wounded, you are the most accomplished.

19. Where you stumble is your gold.

20. When you get your limits, you get your maturity.

21. When you diminish another person, you lose their ability to contribute to you.

22. As long as you have to live inside the tribe, you cannot be a leader.

23. As consciousness rises, significance drops away.

24. The universe is not oppositional, only our minds are.

25. It is all, all working.

26. It's easier to ride the horse in the direction he's going.

27. It is not about me. It may have something to do with me, but it is not about me—or my value. Nor is it about you—or your value.

28. Do not assign emotional responsibility to another. They don't cause it—they only occasion it.

29. Gathering evidence: the way in which we organize our resistance.

30. Get the debt out of relationship.

31. Relationship will not fill my gap (as that solution becomes the problem).

32. There is a difference between taking a stand and being a stand.

33. Position creates opposition. When I take a position, I have to defend it.

34. Context determines content.

35. Attachment produces dependence, dependence produces complaint. You can't get to satisfaction from complaint.

36. Complaint is an abdication of responsibility.

37. Expectation shuts it down.

38. Love is the recognition of the equal in the other.

39. People are miraculous surprises.

40. Sometimes you eat the bear, and sometimes the bear eats you.

"What's So" Letter to Michael Naumer

Michael Naumer
October 21, 1942 - May 4, 2001

SITTING IN YOUR BLACK canvas director's chair, tilting your head, cocking an eyebrow and wiggling your right foot, you listened. You had us raise our hands and stand to speak. No moving the chairs, sitting in a circle, cross-coaching, or helpers in the room. This was all part of the course—a way for us to see ourselves—to see our resistance and our positions. You didn't care if we liked you; that's not why you were there.

For three days you talked about relationship, spirituality, and death. You talked about choice, space, service, and enrollment. You spoke about monogamy and sex, about *what's so* and *what's possible*. You told us your childhood incident, and helped us decipher ours. You talked about Oscar Ichazo, Werner Erhard, and Gurdjeiff. You talked a *lot*. Your raspy voice still follows me around in the back seat of my mind.

Changing the name of the course from the *Mind of Love* to *Beyond the Game,* you spoke of concepts I never gave much thought to: reality and logic, identity and ego, value and debt. You spoke of commitment, trust, choice, and attachment. You told us, "Trying to work things out in your relationship without having worked your stuff out with your parents is like trying to fix the sink when the stove is broken," and "Do you want to be right, or do you want to be effective?" and "The mind is a dangerous neighborhood; don't go in there alone."

You told on yourself, made us laugh, and ended your stories with, "You know, like that." You taught me that everything is important, and nothing is significant. You showed me that I am the projector in my life, not the actor—that things are happening *for* me, not *to* me. You helped me see myself when I couldn't, showing me my mechanisms, structures, and defenses. You helped me turn my pointed index finger around to myself, to see *my* part.

The course was about transformation. *Beyond the Game* was a higher game: chess, not checkers. The objective was self-recognition, and you deemed that the purpose of relationship was not to make oneself happy, but a useful vehicle for seeing oneself. By the end of the weekend we got it. Then we stayed on for the nine-week graduate courses, missing *The Simpsons* on Tuesday nights to be in class.

While leading the October weekend, you thought something was wrong with your contacts so you went to your eye doctor. It turned out to be a tumor. Losing your sight in your left eye, you nearly lost your voice too. It was lung cancer, which finally explained the constant clearing of your throat. By chance, your next graduate course was about death. Previously you'd chosen not to deal with the topic as you felt you couldn't speak to it. But there are no accidents, and when you calmly announced your prognosis to the group, you remarked, "How perfect. Now I have something to say." The doctors gave you four to six months; you made it seven. You taught the January course, and then one in April. Swamped with pain and struggling to breathe, you made it through the three days. From somewhere, you found the strength to stand and give your gifts. You were a higher possibility, and the final course radiated with an amazing grace.

Years before, your teacher gave you a large copper distilling can, given to him by his teacher, and the last time we were together, you passed it on to me. Seated, facing me at your glass dining room table, holding my hands in yours, you told me you were sorry that we hadn't had more fun together. I didn't know you were saying goodbye. I smiled a small smile and whispered through tears, "Maybe next time around." Two days later, no longer able to eat or sleep and bent in pain, for the final time you put on your dress slacks, silk shirt, and struggled with the laces on your black leather shoes. While you were still able to be "at choice" you slowly made your way to the backyard, lay down on a blanket in the grass, and ended your life with a cocked pistol.

Like you said, "Sometimes you eat the bear, and sometimes the bear eats you."

Michael, I miss talking with you on the phone, miss you calling me, *"Hey, beauty,"* miss our friendship and your laugh. My love for you is deep, my gratitude and appreciation boundless, your contribution and the difference you made profound. Thank you.

May 2001

MY SISTER LIZ

YESTERDAY I FOUND OUT that she was dying. I know, thousands of people die every day—but they're not my sister. She's had this constant wracking cough for three months and we finally convinced her to go to a doctor. The first one said it was allergies and sent her home with nasal spray. When the cough persisted, she got a second opinion: pneumonia and antibiotics, then a third diagnosis: tuberculosis, then a fourth: Valley Fever. Finally she saw her husband's cancer specialist. The tests came in yesterday.

The picture of her right lung shows it filled with snowballs of thousands of tiny white threads, the biopsy confirming adenosarcoma, cancer of the soft tissue. Last week our hope was that it hadn't spread beyond her one lung. But it has: it's in the lung's outer lining and in the back of her ribs; it may be in her brain, the part of her body she most values. How ironic. My sister is smarter than anybody I know, except maybe her husband. She and Tony argue and compete for who knows more—which date, who's right, what's fact—and there isn't anything they don't know something about. They collect trivia and knowledge like others collect tea sets and clocks. I told her no need to worry, even if half her brain cells disappeared, she'd still be smarter than the rest of us.

How does my sister feel about dying? During the day she's matter-of-fact about it. As she walked up her long wide driveway lined with lemon trees and date palms to get her newspaper this morning, she passed her neighbor.

"How's it going?"

"Aingh," she replied, then added in afterthought, "I have lung cancer."

"They have cures for that today," he said.

"Not for what I have," she tossed over her shoulder, scooping up her paper and turning back down her shaded path.

How do I feel about her dying? Sometimes, I too am matter-of-fact. I believe when we die, when we leave our body, our soul survives. I don't know where it goes or what happens; maybe we come back and get to do this all over again. Other times, when I'm not so matter-of-fact, when I think about her death and try to imagine her not here, my heart rends. Liz doesn't cry, so I cry for us both.

My sister believes that when we die, that's it. She wants this huge headstone with two carved angels and three pictures of herself at different ages on it so people won't forget her. I told her I didn't think all that many will be lined up to visit it, especially if she didn't start being a little nicer. Liz has a bite, which is partly what I love about her. She's the only person I know who tells the truth about everything, to everyone, at any time. Well, she thinks it's the truth anyway and usually she's right, but it does rile some.

I'm one of the few who escapes her tongue, partly because I fold so easily around her. She loves me, so she's tender with my feelings. It's impossible not to love someone who loves you that much. I can't imagine what it will be like without her. Who will call me every week just to talk? Who will I phone three times a day to help me with my family memoir writings, to tell me I made this part up, that I better not put that part in because it will hurt our brother's feelings, then give me a lesson on homesteading or weirs or the Civil War? Who will I dial when I just want someone to agree with me, or I want to be heard, or I want someone to tell me the truth? Oh, it's not like I don't have others like her in my life—but they're not her. I'll miss her wicked laugh, scathing wit, and opinionated righteous stubbornness. And I'll miss her love for me. I'm trying not to make her dying about me, about what I won't have, about my loss. I'm doing my best to stay out of that space. I know it doesn't help her.

We don't know how long she has—perhaps just months. But sometimes miracles happen, so I told her not to start giving her stuff away yet. She's planning a big going away celebration; she wants to be there when everyone comes to pay their last respects. Some won't be invited: she hasn't spoken to her oldest daughter in five years, can't abide her brother-in-law, and isn't talking to our sister Claudia. They've all crossed her line and she refuses to forgive them. She demands that none of us tell them she's dying. "I don't want them applauding my demise, singing and cheering and dancing a jig on my grave." I keep my mouth shut about how she danced on Mom's. She doesn't give a whit if things don't get worked out with them before she goes. I'm trying to mind my own business about that one, too.

I told her I'd help pick out her headstone. I don't trust her not to get something too gaudy. But it's her funeral, so if she wants to pick out the biggest, most elaborate marble headstone we can find, she can. Maybe we'll get three angels and have the whole thing special ordered from Italy, like the stunning tile in her new kitchen. She'd like that. I'll phone her about it tomorrow.

2004

FINAL MIGRATION

M Y SISTER LIZ KNEW EVERYTHING about everything, and what she didn't know, she made up. Her library was lined with books about architecture, antique lamps, and art nouveau to tomes on history, the human body, and Henry VIII. She also had every field guide on flora, fauna, and all things feathered.

Liz was an avid birdwatcher and the aristocratic and ancient crane was her favorite. A "craniac," she could tell you everything about their habits and habitats, their migration patterns, and their courting rituals. She even knew their mating calls. The birds inspired her, weaving their nests into her daily living. A life-size bronze statue stood sentry at her front door. A delicately feathered watercolor flew on her plaster walls. Cranes perched on her shelves, danced on her Japanese robe, and winged across her glass lampshade.

Each fall, thousands of greater sandhills streak across the Pacific flyway, migrating in families to feed and roost in the safety of the Central Valley wetlands near the Sacramento River. They are one of the world's largest birds, the males standing at a stately five feet tall with a seven-foot wingspan. They are long-legged, long-necked and bustle-bodied, sporting ash gray plumage, a black chiseled bill, sleek white cheeks, and a bald red crown. Their trumpeting can be heard for miles. Between feeding and roosting, they dance this peculiar choreographed avian ballet: first one crane steps out slowly, then a second, the tempo picks up, and soon the whole flock is hopping and bowing—wing-flourishing and stick-tossing in wild rap-like abandon. My sister loved their elaborate floorshow, cackling her delight.

In February, Liz was diagnosed with Stage IV lung cancer. In September, she had experimental surgery at the UC Davis Cancer Clinic in Sacramento. Two weeks later, she came to stay with me. Pneumonia set in and I took her back to the hospital. Three days later, she died.

Just after she took her final breath in that cool early morning, her husband Tony stepped outside to call the family. Dialing his cell phone, there was an overhead cacophony of long drawn-out bugling and clanging so loud he was unable to converse. Looking up, his irritation turned to slack-jawed wonder. A feathered cortege of two hundred greater sandhills passed directly over his wife's top floor hospital room in single and vee formation, first one string, then another behind the first, then another behind them, then another, and another, necks extended, legs and tails outstretched, the slow rhythmic beating of their wings vibrating the crisp October sky, incessantly declaring GAROOO-A-A, GAROOO-A-A.

As is their nature, the whole flock trumpets most raucously when concerned or alarmed. As was her nature, Liz was probably disturbing their flight pattern on her way out. Or maybe she was joining them on their migratory trek. Or perchance, the winged ones knew she was ready and arrived to escort their friend in style, blessing my 64-year-old sister with an exquisite tribute and a final accompaniment.

October 2004

Reincarnation

Elizabeth Ann Duchi
1939 - 2004

SIXTY-FOUR YEARS AGO my middle sister was born:
Elizabeth Ann "Betty/Liz" Clemens.
She was married 46 years, had four children, and was
the funniest person I knew.
A year ago she developed a wracking cough.
Eight months ago she was diagnosed with Stage IV lung can-
cer.
Two months ago she was accepted in an experimental cancer
treatment, her only possible hope.
Three weeks ago she had lung surgery for the making of a
vaccine from her own cells.
Two weeks ago she came to stay with me.

We talked, laughed, told stories, and had a few visitors.
We were anxious and we were scared.
We slept a little, ate a little, cried a little.
I bathed her body, changed her clothes, combed her hair, and
rubbed her swollen ankles.
I brought her food and water and pills and tissues and oxygen
tanks and blankets and love.

I was washing her feet.
She said I would not come back as a cockroach.
I said I didn't think you believed in reincarnation.
She said she must be getting religion.

A week ago Liz took a turn for the worse.
Four days ago I drove her back to the hospital in Sacramento.
  She had pneumonia.
Each day her daughter Julie phoned me and said Liz was getting weaker.
This morning my sister died.

She simply had no breath left in her. I think she was too tired
  to be scared—and I know she was too frail to go on.

Tomorrow my son and I will meet my brother and his wife in
  Carmel and drive to Liz's home in Fallbrook.
The next day there will be a small family gathering.
The day after that,
    and the day after that,
    and the day after that,
    we will celebrate her life.
One day at a time.

October 2004

To My Wife-In-Law

REBECCA, THE BEST THING that happened to our family was you. How could I not care for someone who loved my children as much as I did.

You became my wife-in-law and the boys' other mother. You filled in pieces that Bob and I didn't have the ability to bring. I became the father and you, the mother. You brought the fun, the Easter baskets, and laughter. I brought the rules, household chores, and curfews.

You made sure I got child support, and when you learned I was getting $150 a month, you had Bob double it, and a few years later, double it again. You were a much better wife to Bob than I ever could have been. You had patience and a way with him that I did not. You worked around him. I butted up against him, busily making him incompetent and wrong; we only made it for five years. You remained married to him for eighteen, and now that you are remarried with a child of your own, your new family has become part of ours.

In the beginning, you worked with Bob at the carpet store, and then moved in with him. You were good to the kids. At a time in my life when I was trying to get Country Fresh started, I went to you and asked if you would take Jon for me, just for a while, just until I could get my feet on the ground, and I would like to see him every weekend and please make it okay for him and that it would just be temporary. Matt was starting at Moon Valley School, so he was taken care of during the day.

The hardest thing I've ever done was parting with Jon for those two months. It was so painful for both of us. It was too hard to say goodbye and bring him back or visit him each weekend, so my visits got further apart. You drove him to My School in the morning and when you got to the Washoe House, the two of you would sing, "Wash your hands, wash your face, wash yourself at the Washoe House." You couldn't tell me how much he missed me because you knew it would break my heart.

Jon still had ear infections, and they got worse. Just to prove a point, Bob gave him milk because he didn't believe that both Jon and Matt were lactose intolerant. Each time they stayed with you and Bob, they'd come home with a cold followed by an ear infection. You said, "Well, Bob is Bob," and never expected him to behave any differently.

When Jon was in the seventh grade and Matt a freshman in high school, you planned a trip for the five of us to Mexico.

"Are you nuts? I'm not spending three weeks with Bob, nor am I interested in sharing a hotel room with two teenagers for that length of time. I don't like kids that age."

"Come on, it will be fun," you said. "Bob will lie on the beach and drink beer all day, the boys can play basketball and fish, and we can shop and sightsee," you said. "We'll spend Christmas and New Years in Oaxaca for the festivals, then we'll hang out on the beaches of Zihuatanejo and Ixtapa through New Year's. We'll have a great time," you said.

You talked all of us into it. Then it dawned on me what people would think.

"Look Bob, when people ask, say I'm your sister. They aren't going to get this otherwise. It will be easy, we all have the same last name."

One Southern woman travelling with her two granddaughters got wise, however. After watching and listening to us for a bit, she arched her eyebrows and drawled, "Well now, just how *are* all of you related?"

I looked her right in the eye, raised one eyebrow, and drawled back, "Bah marriage."

We sat in the bleachers together at the boys' baseball and basketball games. You bought them matching cowboy shirts, helped with their college, and stood with us when Matt got married. We spent nearly every holiday together. You live in Canada now, too far for frequent visits, but close enough to be in my heart.

In 1993, I did the Sterling Women's Weekend. You did too. So did my friend Cindy, along with Kristin, Barbara, both Shirleys, Kathy, Jean, Mary, Julie, Lisa, and about fifty other women I knew. We have many women in our lives. After doing that weekend, I understood why I'm not married. And don't intend to be. I do better in my working relationships with men, and have had five great work husbands over the years: Art, Ron, Michael, and two Charlies. I helped run an alternative school, I took on the role of managing and partnering in two real estate companies, and assisted in two long-term coaching endeavors. I had boyfriends to sleep with, quite a few over the years, so it appears. I didn't have to marry someone just to have sex. I did that once.

In the summer of 1994, you and I traveled to Italy with Sandra and her family. We rented a car to meet them in Florence. I was in charge of the map. Florence was in big letters, but the road signs all said Firenze. After circling the city for an hour, you figured it out. A few days later we hooked up with Matt in Milan. He'd been traveling for several months after graduating from college, and when we met up with him, he'd been hitchhiking for days. The hotel nearly didn't let him in because he looked like a vagrant. He was happy to see us and even happier for a bed and a shower. We hiked Cinque Terre, ate pasta and clams to die for, and shopped the flea markets. Shopping rules, according to the boys: "It has to be fragile, expensive, bulky, heavy, and *totally* useless." Sandra and I wanted to buy a matching pair of bronze angels that weighed a ton, but we didn't have enough *lire* on us and her mother wouldn't lend us any money; she thought it was a ridiculous purchase. You bought a complete set of dishes from Deruta and had them shipped home. When you split up with Bob, he got the credit card bill and you got the dishes: I thought you were brilliant. When I split, I got the kids, a 1950 Dodge pickup, and the red couch from Mexico. I'd have rather had the dishes... and the kids, of course.

You left Bob shortly after that trip, but remained a part of our family. You asked me to stand as your witness when you married Dennis. The small town of Ridgecrest, where you both grew up, was a bubble of a bowling-alley-and-beer mentality, and your friends couldn't wrap their arms around that one. You had Lesley soon after. She was adorable and funny. I put ice cubes down the back of her jammies. She called me Cathysevenau, as if that was my first name.

We have Christmas with your new family and you have Thanksgiving with us. Bob comes, too. You share your mother, Pat, with me. At my Thanksgiving table one year, Bob was at one end, I was at the other, and seated on one side were you, Dennis, Pat, Lesley, and your brother. On the opposite side were Matt and Jon, my niece Julie, Dennis' daughter Becky, and Bob's fourth wife. Bob started in on the embezzler in the family (who was not present) and I held up my hand like a traffic cop at a crosswalk, "Look, it's Thanksgiving. Could we not do this at the dinner table?"

He stabs his fork in the air and says, "Oh, so you live in some fairyland and think time heals all wounds?"

I paused two beats and retorted, "Well, darling, you certainly wouldn't be sitting here if I didn't."

Everyone busted up, especially Pat, who thought Bob had said, "So you think time wounds all heels?" This made everyone except Bob laugh even harder, since in this case, it was pretty much the same thing.

That was the year Pat suggested we order the whole kit and caboodle from Safeway, and go for a hike on Thanksgiving morning instead.

I was shocked. "Can we do that?"

"Of course we can," she said.

Your mother had style. We ordered it the day before and picked up everything that morning: stuffed turkey, mashed potatoes, gravy, green beans with onion rings, sweet potatoes, cranberry sauce, pineapple and marshmallow salad, and three pies. Then we hid the boxes, and no one knew. The boys went on and on, saying it was the best Thanksgiving dinner I'd ever made.

When your brother died, the pastor failed to show, so you asked me to take his place. I was so nervous that I can't remember how it went, other than looking for support at the woman in the back coordinating the microphone and giving me hand directions as to what to do next, watching your mother nodding in grief, and everyone crying, I spoke about him as best I could. I think it went okay.

When your mother was dying, you called and asked me to come down immediately to be with you both at the hospital in Palm Springs. It was too big for you to do by yourself. I was there within hours. I sat with Pat to give you a break. We held hands and looked into one another's eyes and communicated with finger pressures, saying we loved each other and that it was okay and not to be scared. You were her hospital advocate, and one of your biggest concerns was that in more than a week she'd not had a bowel movement. When I returned home a couple of days later, Lesley called in great relief.

"She pooped!" It was headline news.

You brought me friendship, support, and love. You kept Bob out of my hair. You loved our sons. The only time you ever got mad at me was when we were on a street corner in Spain, you were studying the map, and I asked you which way we were going. You snapped, "How the f*** would I know? We've only been here two hours. Why am I always in charge of the directions?"

Tearing up, I said, "Well, I don't think you want me to be in charge." It was my birthday that day, and at lunch, you apologized and gave me a pair of gold angel earrings.

Thank goodness you were in our life while the boys were growing up. Between the two of us, we made a good mother. I am grateful that you are still in my life! We've been related for more than forty years. When it's time to leave, maybe we do it together, giving each other a last smooch and going over the cliff like Thelma and Louise or Butch and the Sundance Kid. Although, as I'm not all that adventuresome, maybe we just call it a day, have one last cup of tea and a cookie, kiss one another goodbye, and turn out the lights.

LAST PIECE
OF CHOCOLATE

KIM JOINED OUR OFFICE as an agent in 1994. As it turned out we had a lot in common: we both loved real estate, ice cream, and dark chocolate. In 2002 she became a partner in my real estate practice: she took over showing property to my clients—which meant I no longer got lost wandering around town looking for streets that were not where I remembered them—organized much of the paperwork, and dealt with the details of short sales when they became the bane of our existence.

Kimmy was diplomatic, charming, and easygoing. The one thing in her way was her indecisiveness, but she made up for it with her determination and spunk. It just wasn't Kim's nature to be decisive. "I can't help it that I'm wishy-washy," she told me, "I'm a Libra." As our offices adjoined, I could hear her talking to clients. I'd roll my eyes and wonder how she ever nudged anyone to make a decision. The difficulty in making up her mind could take hold of her, even in mundane choices. Shopping was fraught with internal conflict, so she returned much of what she bought. She admitted once that what she liked most about shopping was returning everything. During the holidays a couple of seasons ago, the back of her SUV was crammed with boxes.

"What is all this?" I asked her.

"I'm taking it all back to the store."

"Why?"

"I don't know, I couldn't decide if any of it was really what I wanted."

It worked out perfectly for me. I did my Christmas shopping right there in our parking lot.

For ten years Kim and I were joined at the hip. We made a great team, filling in one another's gaps; I kept her on course and she kept me on track. Many mornings she'd call from the office and ask the same thing, "What are you doing?" In the middle of family research on Ancestry or Find A Grave, I'd answer, "I'm working on dead people," and she'd bark back, "Get down here. They're dead. They'll wait."

Then life took a sharp turn. In June of 2011, Kim was diagnosed with Stage IV lung cancer. Her first doctor sent her home with no hope and little time. A second doctor said, "Wait a minute. You're young, healthy, and in great shape—you fight this!" She followed that advice, dumping her first doctor. A combination of chemo, daily injections, rounds of doctors, batteries of tests, bottles of pills, tanks of oxygen, prayers, holy water, bodywork, herbal remedies, food from friends, buckets of love, and a fair amount of laughter—along with her great spunk, mettle, and optimism—had Kim outlive the first doctor's projections by more than a year.

In those months she recovered enough to return to work. She wasn't kickboxing, but her breathing was better and her color and smile had returned. She celebrated her sixty-fifth and sixty-sixth birthdays, ventured to the Century 21 Annual Convention in New Orleans, and with her husband Dan took an Alaskan cruise and celebrated their nineteenth wedding anniversary. She was able to be with her children and grandchildren to celebrate birthdays and holidays. And every afternoon she slowly swam with Dan in the warm water of their lap pool, enjoying the hummingbirds hovering in the yard and watching the same two crows holding court on the branch of their flowering cherry.

Then the cancer spread. The pain in her bones and the inability to breathe sent her back to the hospital where, for three weeks, her family stayed with her around the clock. I saw Kim twice in her last week. On my final visit, we had time alone while the family conferred with doctors. I sat as close as I could without disturbing anything as she was hooked up to monitors, an IV, and had two oxygen contraptions on her face.

"Tell me what's going on at the office," she said. I leaned in closer to hear her. "What happened at the meeting today? Did you get the names of the mentor families for the Thanksgiving dinners? And after a long pause, "and my view clients, did you reach them?" Kim's labored breathing, the oxygen mask, and her small continuous cough made it hard to understand her, and her talking made her cough worse. I told her everything and everyone was taken care of, not to fret.

She faded in and out over the next hour. Then came a moment when she looked straight at me. In a small, clear voice she said, "There's dark chocolate here in the room. Want some?"

"Yeah," I said. "How about you, you want some?"

"Yeah," she whispered back.

I broke off a small piece. Kim struggled to get the chocolate past her mask, and I gently wiped off the leftover smudges on her fingers. We closed our eyes and as heaven melted in our mouths I thought: *when I'm dying, I hope that the last thing that passes my lips will be a piece of good dark chocolate.*

I knew this was the last time I would be with her, but neither of us could say goodbye. She didn't want to leave and I didn't want her to go, so we left it at that. Two days later, on the eighth of November, my friend Kim took a final breath, quietly slipping out of this life.

2012

A CHICKEN STORY

"WILL YOU LEAVE ME SOMETHING in your will? No one's ever left me anything—mainly because most of my family didn't have much to leave anyone—so just once," I said, "I'd like to inherit something."

We were sitting in the shade of Kim's backyard, crunching thin slices of apples with jack cheese. There were times when she didn't have the energy to do much, so I'd wander over (we lived three blocks from one another) to keep her company and make her laugh. And there were a couple of times I stalked over to drag her off the couch to go outside for a walk because she was freaked out, hiding under a blanket all day on her couch. The corner at the end of her block was a long way for her to go, so she'd take my arm and we'd take our time, and we both felt better afterwards. This day happened to be a good day and we were swapping sex, drugs, and rock and roll stories. Kim had a fascinating past: her dad produced television shows so she knew a lot of stars and did some acting as a kid; then she became a flower child and travelled all over Europe in a Volkswagen van, then lived on the little island of Formentera. Her stories were WAY more interesting than mine, and we laughed until our teeth rattled loose. We promised one another we'd never tell a soul and take the stories to our graves. No one needs that much information about either of us. Ever.

So Kim says, "What would you like?"

"I've been thinking about it," I said, "and I'd like one of your chickens."

She had a collection of ceramic, metal, and wooden fowl in her kitchen, all pretty cute. Trish, our friend, co-worker, gardening, and interior decorator queen who helped Kim and Dan design their remodel on Patten Street, had found a few of them for her.

"And if I go before you, which is a possibility but not likely considering the circumstances," I said, "what would you like of mine?" She said she'd think about it. Then we rambled on about our parents, siblings, kids, and grandchildren, about being Jewish and Catholic, about books and food and work. Then we had ice cream.

A few months later Kim's lung cancer came back with a vengeance. On the bad days we'd just sit together, the weight of it all too heavy for either of us to carry by ourselves. We didn't talk about her dying as she had no intention of doing so, but my friend was sensible and had all her affairs in order, just in case. I wasn't about to rain on her parade by having any death conversations and anyway, she simply wasn't going to go there. I didn't want her to leave either, but I also did not want her to suffer so, and from where I sat, things weren't looking good. It was the inability to breathe, the fluid in her lungs, and the pain in her back that caused most of her suffering. She ended up back in the hospital, where I got to be with her twice more.

Two days after she died, her husband Dan called. "I'm lying here in bed, reading Kim's will. It's interesting. She left you something."

"Really," and after a puzzled pause I asked, "What?"

"She left you a chicken. It says, *Catherine and Trish, pick a chick.* Why would she leave you two a chicken?"

I smiled, "Because she loved us," and then hooted, "Now that's a good one! How perfect that she got the last laugh!"

November 2012

A MID-CENTURY
CLASSIC

O
N MY LAST MARKER birthday (sixty-fifth) I muddled
over penning my obit, my epitaph, or a newspaper ad.
My own obituary was too weird to write. My epitaph
was a no-brainer...

> CATHERINE FRANCES SEVENAU
> 1948 — TBD
> HOW DID I GET HERE?

Since I've been in real estate forever, the ad copy was also
easy:

Celebrate a Contemporary Mid-Century Classic

This small-town charmer shines with character and a colorful
history. Endowed with good bones on a solid concrete foundation, she is structurally sound in conjunction with notable
internal integrity. Built in 1948, this gem is a prime example
of definitive California architecture, and other than the well-
maintained roof, is in original condition. Despite an outstand-
ing location with gracious curb appeal, her interior is
somewhat dated and shows a bit of wear and tear. No major
complaint or disclosure issues, no plumbing leaks or wiring
problems, no illegal permit or zoning headaches, but does
bear some slight quirks: two partially fogged windows, various rusted hinges, a few loose screws, and several stiff,

creaking doors. There are minor holes in the ceiling (allowing hot air to escape), along with dinky wall dents here and there. No termites or beetles, but possibly squirrels in the attic. Well-tended and generally low maintenance, though can be temperamental depending on the weather. Recently smudged for ghosts. For quick turnaround, an authentic plastic St. Joseph statue is buried upside down in the backyard. Comes fully insured with newly-minted historical designation. Well-documented archival background information on request.

August 2013

ON THE
WOO-WOO SIDE

TWO EVENTS OCCURRED on my trip to Southern California last weekend that might catch your attention. The first was at the funeral for Kay's (high school friend) mom. Family and friends drove in caravan with a police escort to the cemetery after having the service at the Mormon Church up the road. As I'm standing behind where the family is seated, I notice "Memory Garden" imprinted at the top of the shade tent. Now don't ask why, but I ask Kay's cousin standing next to me, "What town are we in?" He says "Brea." I turn to him and out of my mouth comes, "My mother is buried in this cemetery," and I turn and look behind us at the buildings on the hill, "up there."

I was at Memory Garden in 1968 when my siblings and I gathered to inter my mother's ashes, and again with my brother a dozen years ago when I was working on a family memoir. Considering who I am in the world, I'm amazed that I somehow knew where I was. I took leave of the group and slipped away for a moment to find her niche, way up high. I snapped a picture and asked her to watch over Kay's mom, now that they were neighbors, and to intervene on my behalf with whoever is mad at me on the other side that keeps holding up the finishing of my book.

After the reception I headed two hours north to Camarillo where I was spending the night at my cousin's, a Chatfield (my grandfather Isaac W. Chatfield was her grandmother's brother). Joanne (age 89) had fallen on her patio nine months ago, cracking her head on the cement, and never came home. While in recovery she broke her leg falling out of her wheelchair, then dementia crept in and stole her mind, too. I was staying with her husband, Lee (also age 89). He sits with her, heartbroken, for three hours every other day as she lies in bed staring at the ceiling, her one broken leg bent over the other.

Joanne had pictures of our ancestors that I'd seen before which Lee was letting me borrow. The only one we couldn't find was a 6 x 14 inch sepia on cardboard (circa 1890) of her grandfather Josiah Small in a Civil War re-enactment. It was not in the boxes we'd gone through.

In the nine months that Joanne had been in the hospital, bills, letters, and magazines had accumulated, taking over their dining room, piled on the table, chairs and floor. I needed a bigger envelope to fit some of the larger pictures in, and Lee went into the garage to look for one. Next to me on the chair about an inch down in a foot high stack, I spotted a thin brown bag that they'd fit in. I slipped it out, hoping it was empty, but found two pictures in it. One of them... hang on... was the missing Josiah Small. It was a Kinko's bag, and on the pictures was a sticky note with my email address. Joanne fell before she could get them to me.

I had no inkling ahead of time about that bag, any more than I had a sense in the beginning that I was in the cemetery where my mother was—but these things happen to me, especially around working on our genealogy or writing my book. I'm quietly led to the next piece I need, and out of the ethers, it appears. It's like a cosmic consciousness opens and allows me in. It used to weird me out, but I've learned not to question grace; now I simply bow to the mystery of it all, filled with awe and appreciation.

September 2014

BLESS THIS MESS

HARDWIRED FOR FORMAL PRAYER, I find myself reciting the *Our Father* when an earthquake hits, and oftentimes at night as I go to sleep. "How weird," I think, stopping in the middle, but then a *Hail Mary* (a woman about whom I hold equally wobbly beliefs), arises to take its place. I surrender, then move on to blessing my family, friends, and then the people who irritate me. Some nights I just cut to the chase and bless the ones I seriously want to hurt. So much for being spiritual.

Both of my grandmothers were Catholic, stubborn, and right. I'm much like them, though I don't know why I still refer to myself as Catholic. I'm addicted to being right (a first cousin to being perfect). Both have a tendency to be corrosive in relationships. Resentment is in our DNA, our cellular memory, creeping through generations, across lines, round the corners and back again. When Grandpa Charlie Chatfield (who had the propensity to err) died, the only thing Grandma Nellie had to say was, "serves the damn fool right," then she buried her wayward husband in an unmarked grave in the non-Catholic section of the cemetery. Now that's angry.

It's hard to restore family grace if there wasn't much there to begin with, though it does make for good storytelling. C'mon, who is going to be captivated by the tales of Catholic farmers with a passel of kids, who worked the same land for generations and never broke the rules? The stories lend stability via my Clemens side (for which I'm exceedingly grateful), but offer little of interest to write about. Fiction is too complicated for me to create, and really, why bother when my

Chatfield, Hoy, and Chamberlin lines teem with an overabundance of characters that supply me with endless material. I'm fascinated by these folks, while at the same time rather appalled at their bad behavior, and couldn't make some of this stuff up if I tried.

I have missing mothers, though they do generally reappear. I have stories that make for compelling page turners: drugs, pills, prison, murder, kidnapping, rape, abortions, child abuse, molestation, neglect, asylums, shock treatments, and suicides. I also have poisonings, cattle thieves, liars, bookies, bettors, bootleggers, embezzlers, moonshiners, and drunks. I have a grandfather who gambled away the ranch (which is one of the reasons Grandma Nellie never forgave Grandpa). I have gay elopements (in May of 1889, Ora Chatfield, age 15, ran off with her cousin Clara Deitrich who was age 28 and the postmistress and general storekeeper of Emma, Colorado... you can look it up), multiple marriages, numerous divorces and a boatload of annulments. I have racism (you'd be horrified; I am), a John Bircher, and a Scientologist. I have an Arcturian, flying saucer abductions, tealeaf reader, spirits, voodoo, and ghosts. And that's just on my mother's side—though I notice that several of us have married into similar lines—cementing our proclivity to chaos. I don't have to ponder what to write about. I have to ponder what NOT to write about.

Most of the hurts siblings nurse against one another stem from when we were little kids. LITTLE KIDS! Little kids who were just being little brats. Those are the wars I wonder about, how things that happened when we were younger than five or six years old can ruin a relationship for life. Really? Like when my sister Liz was dying, she forbade her husband and children to allow Claudia, another sister, to attend the family get-together after her passing. When Claudia found out, you know what her response was? "It's okay. Liz never did like me, ever since we were kids." REALLY???

I bear generations of resentments handed down: siblings suing each other, daughters dancing on graves, parents cutting children out of the will. We like to hang on to things. For whatever reason, there are more than a few of us who don't speak to one another, or if we do, we tread lightly—but that's been going on for years. It's how we keep the home fires burning.

What can I do in the family to counteract our genetic umbrage? I can throw light on it—though writing about certain things tends to irk some when it's too close to home. I can do my part to not perpetuate conflict. I know how hard it is, though. I so often want to slap the other cheek, and I'm not about to easily turn mine. I can counteract it by not living as if we're not connected, and by holding the possibility that things can change. I can choose not to take sides. I can keep an eye on what I'm up to. I can make amends to those my shiv has wounded. "I'm sorry" goes a long way.

I believe in the ineffable power of prayer, though it's presumptuous of me to suppose that I can decipher enough—in the grand scheme of things—to pray for what I think is best. Some say prayers can move mountains. However, that's where my critical thinking raises its hairy head, seeking evidence.

If you pray for rain long enough, it eventually does fall.
If you pray for floodwaters to abate, they eventually do.
The same happens in the absence of prayers.
—Steve Allen (1921 - 2000)

The best I can do is to still my rattling mind, to sit in wonder, silence, and gratitude. To continue to silently recite as a reminder and a comfort: *forgive us our trespasses, as we forgive those who trespass against*—the sacred version of: *let it go, let it go, let it go*—sometimes out of habit, other times with intention. Forgiving someone doesn't mean forgetting what was done, it just means being able to stop pointing fingers and move on. We don't have to have lunch together.

> *If the only prayer you said was thank you,*
> *that would be enough.*
> —Meister Eckhart (1260 - 1328)

Amen.

2015

I Want What I Want When I Want It

I AM SELF-SUFFICIENT and self-supporting, along with self-reliant, self-confident and self-motivated. I can also be self-serving, self-critical, self-centered, self-righteous and perhaps just a wee bit self-absorbed.

I reek of responsibility and good reputation.

I hold dear my anxiety, all the while remaining tethered to my resentment.

Stubborn, I'm like a dog with a bone in its mouth.

I get mired in the details—a known list-maker and lint-picker.

I wanted the badge of busyness so badly, then life got too complicated.

I'm tired: tired of being late, late, late, never feeling that I can possibly get everything done, wearing myself out with my accomplishing, questioning, and searching. I'm feverish with all my thinking, afraid to stop doing... afraid of what might happen if I did.

I have a lot of rules, and a tendency to wear my halo a little tight.

A know-it-all, I can be annoyingly bossy.

I want to be mad. I want to be right. I want to be liked.

I long to have patience immediately.

I can be tight-lipped and stingy, especially with small things.

I get annoyed when you can't, won't, or don't get to the point.

I yearn to have everything neat and tidy, like my sock drawer.

I want to be the boss. (I don't want to be responsible; I just want to be in charge.)

I'm never simply cold, hungry, or tired. Nooo, I'm freezing, starving, or exhausted.

I get cranky if I haven't eaten. (Actually, I get hostile if I haven't eaten.)

I want more than I have and I want things to be different.

I get confused. (I'm *not* the one to ask if you need directions.)

I have a few beliefs no one can talk me out of.

I carry unmet expectations, mostly of myself.

I have an edgy mistrust when it comes to affairs of the heart.

I haven't decided how I feel about God. It's absurd to suppose that He'd choose as His companions for all eternity only those whose sole ambition was to obey. I also no longer believe the stories I've been told about being a blotch on His creation. Who makes up this stuff, anyway?

Am I happy? At times, when I don't let my thoughts and emotions drag me around. Am I learning compassion? Yes, one breath at a time. It's not, however, my strong suit.

I worry less about what I do and more about how I be.

Instead of asking "please" I practice saying "thank you."

What I believe is true for me, so I'm more careful as to what I believe. I also try not to believe everything I think.

I try to be grateful.

I try to be mindful.

I try to surrender.

And sometimes I hit a good lick!

I do the best I can, and then I let it go.

I am that I am, and I know that I'm enough.

I wish that—and this—for my grandchildren, and their children, and theirs:

That they hold dear their genuine curiosity, that they work hard in life to be where they want, and that they joyously experience the miraculous Seven Wonders of the World:
>~to see
>~to hear
>~to touch
>~to taste
>~to feel
>~to laugh
>~to love

I want them to know seventh heaven and the seven seas. I want them to be magnificently fearless, passionate, thankful, and kind. I want them to grow up and be useful, to make a difference, and to lead a life well-lived. And with the greatest of hope, I want them to know peace.

CREDO FOR TODAY

Why am I here? Who am I? What do I believe?
How shall I live my life? Where do I stand?
When do I speak out?

Ten Commitments

1. I shall honor Spirit: my God, your God, their gods, and the god within me.

2. I shall honor my word, and take responsibility for what I speak.

3. I shall rest, honoring a Sabbath time.

4. I shall honor my family, my community, and my beloved biosphere.

5. I shall honor my capacity to kill—and have the common sense, wisdom, and compassion to not commit such an act.

6. I shall honor my sexuality, committing no offense.

7. I shall not steal.

8. I shall tell the truth—and endeavor not to add to chaos, war, or misery.

9. I shall govern my envy of others, refusing to let it dictate my behavior.

10. I shall be grateful, to humbly bow and kneel to the beauty and mystery of it all.

Ten Reminders

1. Clean up my inner litter; this includes not dumping it in my neighbor's yard.

2. Quit carping and complaining, raining my misery on others.

3. Let go of my personal hurts; stop nursing them as if they were my only children.

4. I am not the center of the universe; life is not all about me and what I want.

5. I am connected and interconnected with everything. What I do matters.

6. Accept all of myself, and all of you—our greatness and our pettiness.

7. Be of service to others, and to something greater than myself.

8. Loosen my attachments: to being right, to being liked, to being perfect.

9. Listen to and trust my inner voice, my inner wisdom, and the wisdom of my body.

10. Befriend death and dying.

Why Am I Here? Perhaps ...

I am here to wake up.
I am here to be useful.
I am here to be happy.
I am here to make a difference.
I am here to work out my spiritual dilemmas.
I am here to love.
I am here to create.
I am here to be in this miraculous yet ordinary body.
I am here to realize my birthright as an evolving being.
I am here to remember who I am.

RANTS

A Confused Heart
and a White Train

October 7, 1967 • San Francisco

O N A CLEAR, CRISP OCTOBER DAY, my father escorted me down the carpeted aisle of Holy Name of Jesus, our church in the Sunset.

I looked like a fairy princess, dressed in the white floor-length wedding dress my stepsister wore when she married. It fit like a dream: white lace, cap sleeves, darted at the waist… not a dress I would have chosen, but comely, the train following me, my knees shaking, my lips twitching, my mouth so dry my lips were stuck to my teeth like a fool's tongue on a frozen flagpole. Six-foot-six Father O'Shaughnessy, in his white collar and black robes, smiled his handsome crooked tan smile. Our four bridesmaids (my three high school friends and my niece Debbie, fourteen and stoned) wore matching, full-length, empire-waist coral bridesmaid dresses, holding bouquets of dyed carnations and baby roses. The four ushers (Bob's two school friends and two brothers) dressed in black tails, and Bob, looking baby-faced and nervous, waited for us expectantly at the altar.

It's better that I didn't invite Mom. It would be too hard on Daddy and she would've wrecked this, and besides, I haven't seen her in years and she wouldn't care anyway.

I thought about how hard Marie worked to make this a wonderful wedding, about what it cost and how Daddy used his inheritance money, about how far everyone traveled. I wanted to run—but I didn't make promises lightly; I also didn't want to disappoint everybody. As I peered out from under my veil at 150 people, our families and friends, our parents' friends, Bob's mother... *oh my god, she looks like a leprechaun!* She's got on a green, knee-length, lace-covered dress and matching pantyhose, a green flowered hat and veil, green eye-shadow, holding a green handbag with her feet stuffed into three-inch, dyed-to-match heels barely making her five-feet tall. I was bobbling on the edge of hysteria. I glanced sideways at my father, looking so handsome in his tuxedo; I could smell his lapel flower and his splash of Old Spice. I forgot about Velma (who wasn't particularly thrilled about her little Bobby marrying me) and moved into a silent rant with him.

"How did I get here? How could this be happening? This is your fault! If you hadn't chimed in and nearly knocked your chair over at Bob's birthday dinner party when he announced we were getting married with your "oh no...""

And so, with my family and friends as witnesses—against all my better judgment—with a confused heart, a bowed head, a white train, and a full Mass, I married a boy who had the same thimble-full of common sense that I did.

NEEDLES

WHEN PETER TOLD ME I CHOSE MY MOTHER, I almost fell off the table. Now I liked Peter, but I wasn't so sure about him. The first time I saw him was for pain in my knuckles. My joints were aching and a friend suggested going to him. She'd gotten herbs from him that helped her with her arthritis.

Peter was an acupuncturist. Taking my pulse, he proclaimed, "It's not your joints, it's your liver."

He tried to talk me into lying on the table. He would just put a couple of tiny little needles in my ear lobes and both shoulders, just a little bit, and promised it wouldn't hurt. I'd had enough needles stuck in me to last me forever... no way was I about to lie on that table.

"No, I'll just try the herbs, thanks."

Going back, but now because of shoulder pain, he told me, "It's not your *shoulder*, it's your *kidneys*," and suggested trying the needles again. On my third visit he convinced me that the needles would help, and promised that they wouldn't hurt; I let him, but only three. My shoulder did feel better after the treatment. I kept going back to Peter, and over time he talked me into more and more needles, and then I'm going once a week. Treating me for a respiratory infection it became, "It's not your *lungs*, it's your *heart*," and the needles hurt something fierce this time. I'm screaming and hollering and he's telling me to pipe down, that I'm the worst patient he's ever had and I'm scaring the patient in the adjoining room and I tell him he's the worst doctor I ever had and he doesn't know jack about anatomy and why do the needles hurt so bad this time?

He confessed he'd run out of the tiny ones and thought maybe I wouldn't notice the next size up, and he tried putting them in me a little further, then said that all along he'd barely had them in me and that's why they didn't hurt. *Really?*

I got used to the needles—a little bit. They still hurt, but I saw they weren't going to kill me, and, they did seem to help. I went to Peter for a couple of years. The kicker was the day he said the pain I was having in my knuckle was not my knuckle, it was my mother. Then he proceeds to tell me I chose her.

"Oh, *please*. Why would I ever choose *her*? I didn't choose my mother. I was confused. I got in the wrong line. It wasn't *my* fault." I was now less sure of him than I'd ever been.

There came a time I was in for some female issues, and after a couple of treatments he spoke with a quiet seriousness, "You came into my meditation last night, and I saw a black spot on your ovaries. I have a question for you. What happened to you when you were nine?"

Without missing a beat I said, "My brother-in-law Bobby molested me."

"Did you ever tell anyone?"

"No, it only happened once, he didn't hurt me, and at the time I had no idea what had happened, but I knew it was wrong. I didn't know what sex was. I also didn't think it was important, but I made sure I wasn't alone with him again."

"Cath, this is lodged in your body and is creating health issues in you. I want you to do two things. When you go home, I want you to lie on the floor, make your knees into a tent, put you hands over your stomach, close your eyes, and breathe slowly. Take your time, but go in there and see what comes up for you. I also want you to share it with your family."

So I did. What happened next scared me. I followed his instructions, and when I started breathing deeply and tried imagining the spot, I rolled over into the fetal position and was shaking so uncontrollably that I began to cry. I was shocked that I had so much energy stored in me around this. So I stayed with it as long as I could, and when I couldn't take it any more, I got up sobbing and crawled into bed.

The next week I called my siblings, then I phoned my children. I started with Liz and I told her the story. Miss Blabbermouth called Carleen before I could get to her, so Carleen was hurt that I didn't call her first. They both said it figured, as neither had any love loss for Bobby. My brother, after listening uncomfortably, said he was sorry I'd gone through that. Then I called Claudia, who was married to Bobby at the time it happened. She was just fifteen, he was nineteen and in the Navy, stationed at Barber's Point on Oahu. Mom and I moved there when he was transferred there as she thought she should be near Claudia because she was so young. Of course she's the one that let Claudia get married at fourteen in the first place.

Claudia's response, considering the players involved, was interesting. "I don't believe you."

"I don't care if you believe me, that's not the point of the call. I was simply instructed to share this with my family, so I am. And I'm curious why this might be such a surprise to you; he was screwing you when you were thirteen."

"When did it happen? Where were you? Where were Mom and I?"

"I was with Bobby at your apartment and you and Mom had probably gone to the commissary for cigarettes. I don't know where you where, but you weren't there."

"How many times did in happen?"

"Once."

"Do you remember it?"

"In detail, Claudia, in slow motion detail."

"Tell me."

So I did. At the end of the story, she says, "I believe you."

"Claudia, I don't care if you believe me or not. I'm simply reporting. I don't want to have health issues over this so I'm just doing what my doctor suggested I do."

"You know, when we lived in Hawaii, Mom sent you to a psychiatrist. You were having recurring nightmares of a man standing at the top of the stairs, holding a gun. You'd also gone into the hospital again with another bout of vomiting spells. I think the psychiatrist suspected, and he told Mom that maybe you needed to live in a different environment. After the school year ended, you went to stay with Carleen."

"I remember the hospital, and I remember the psychiatrist. I remember the sandbox, the inkblots, and me sitting in the big black swivel chair thinking he had the wrong one of us in there. I don't remember the nightmares."

Then I made the calls to my sons. Both of them had the same response:

"Where does he live?"

I could tell by the tone of their voices what they had in mind.

"You're sweet, but there's no need to defend my honor. He lives in Mississippi, he's an old man now, and it was a long time ago."

I thank Peter for the work he did with me around this, and thank myself for having the courage to trust him. I have a childhood history of being hospitalized for malnutrition and dehydration from vomiting spells, of having my veins collapse in my arms and on the back of my hands so they had to use my legs and ankles for the IV, of needles snapping, of my arms and legs being taped down on boards so the needles wouldn't pull out, and after four or five days of being strapped to a hospital bed, of only being given ice chips to suck on every few hours, of then having the tape ripped off, ripping out all my hair on my arms or my legs. I've had horrible experiences from dreadful shots of Novocain, having nearly every tooth in my mouth jackhammered and drilled by Nazi dentists. I have memories of being tortured from having over a hundred moles burned off my body—some with anesthetic, some not—the smell of my skin burning making me sick.

So don't tell me about needles—and about how they don't hurt. I have plenty of evidence that they nearly did me in when I was a kid. There were times it was so bad that I'd leave my body and watch from above; it was safer up there. I also don't remember anyone at my side to hold my hand, to comfort me and tell me not to be afraid, to assure me that I wouldn't die.

Odd, isn't it... who knew that the thing I was most afraid of as a child, the weapons that caused me the most pain, would be the very instruments to help cure my body as an adult?

Cosmic Patience

I HADN'T SAID A WORD the first three days; I had nothing to add and was seeing plenty about myself simply sitting on the floor and listening—how I still need to control my environment so I'm not too hot, not too cold, not too tired—and how hard it is for me to relax and not believe my discomfort will lead to my certain death. This is why I'm so rigid at times; it takes a lot of armor to protect myself in my world. I was in a four-day workshop on being present. I observed myself slow down, heard my mind quiet, felt my body relax. Then I watched myself undo it all by getting riled by a young man—who in the beginning I felt only mildly irritated by, and by the end wanted to slap silly, rattle his brains, and then choke to death. I hate the packages my lessons comes in.

This kid—a slumping question mark dressed in a shapeless brown hair-shirt of a sweater—said nothing in three days other than he was angry but didn't know *why* he was angry, and that he wanted to kill someone and then he'd actually describe how he'd do it, and that he was sad but didn't know *why* he was sad, and then he'd cry and say he just wanted to express his sadness *and* his anger but didn't know how, so he mostly sat there and whined or writhed on the floor like a sniveling worm in tears and… you get the picture. Any previous compassion I had warped into fantasies of murder. By his thirteenth time in front of the room, (okay so maybe I'm exaggerating, maybe it was only his twelfth) my being-held-hostage thing kicked in and I snapped. At the break I took my frustration to the teacher, a perfectly normal looking guy in a casual shirt and slacks who still has bruises on his body from my fingernails digging into him, threatening that if he allowed this to continue, either he or this kid would be dead. Suggesting I bring my complaint to the room, he said I would also be speaking for others, and yes, perhaps he *had* let him go on a bit too long this time. *THIS TIME?* Oh please.

I attempted to speak up before I went into a total meltdown but I wasn't called upon and I was being polite. Then it was too late. You see, this was a SPIRITUAL GROUP and where I was headed was anywhere but spiritual. After the break (which I spent outside in the gray drizzle stomping and raging for twenty minutes) I was the first to take the microphone. Wild horses couldn't have stopped me. Composed, even-spoken, direct—and in front of ninety people—I blasted this brat, then warned him with what I would do if he dared come to the front of the room, ask for the microphone, or be ever so stupid as to even raise his hand until he had a complete thought, was willing to perhaps at least get to *some* point, or had something to contribute that was even mildly useful. "No more complaining, whining, or drama from you. None. Or you will be very, very sorry. I will hurt you. I promise." The room softened and he was the only person in my vision. For the first time, he was sitting up straight. It was fortunate as it lessened my intense desire to stomp over and kick the crap out of him.

When I said everything I had to say, I waded through the sea of people to my chair. The teacher, laughing, said, "Were you part of the encounter groups in the 60s?" I turned halfway and said, slowly, "*No....* I was *working* in the sixties."

Several hands shot up. This kid's girlfriend, who I personally think is as screwed up as he is simply because she sees something in this little dweeb, glared at me and spit, "I feel nothing but hate for that woman." Then a second disgruntled bliss-bunny demanded to know if the teacher was going to let me get away with what I just did. My reaction at one time would have been, *oh, oh, I'm in trouble*. This time my internal retort was, *kiss my ass*. The teacher's rejoinder was for them to mind their own business—this had nothing to do with them and any reaction they had was their stuff. His response to the rest of the room was, although I may not have done it very elegantly, I'd hit the nail on the head and this young man might want to listen to what I had to say—maybe he could learn something. I knew when I returned to my chair and at the dinner break that I'd spoken for a good part of the room because the majority fervently thanked me under their breaths. I must admit I do appreciate people agreeing with me: it validates I'm not the only one, it validates my righteousness, it also validates my rightness—and—my right to speak. A few weren't triggered and simply witnessed what was going on. Frankly, I don't know if I want to live my life that flatlined, having cosmic patience, willing to pay attention for hours to someone who is a candidate for shock treatment or a lobotomy. This is why I don't teach—they don't let you slap the whack-jobs.

So what else did I observe? That I'm weary of workshops where I pay $500 to see myself; I could stay home and give members of my family ten bucks each and save a bucket load; they're happy to point out my blind spots. I could hang out with my sons if I want to get triggered. I could look for answers inside rather than out there. It's just so overpopulated in me that I can't hear over the din: my mother's in here, my father's in here, my sisters and brother, the rest of my family, my ancestors, my teachers, the Pope, Judge Judy, Miss Manners, the Queen of Hearts and the Mad Hatter, my beliefs, structures, entanglements, my attachments and opinions, my superiority, my inferiority, my past, my future, all the stuff I make up, all the stuff I drag around, and all the stuff I hang onto. The Gestapo is in here too and they can't even break it up. In addition, I see how my unwillingness to surrender, my internal critic, external judge, and my resentful ego can entirely, totally, and utterly run my show.

And so, thank you Lord—I get to be present with me. I'm grateful. I could have come back this time as that kid. It's hard enough being in my morally superior, scolding body; I can only imagine what it must be like to be in his.

April 2004

Postscript: I attended an evening course a couple of months later (it took me that long to recover) led by the same teacher, and the slumping question mark just happened to be sitting in front of me, though he looked like a different person. There are no accidents. At the break I tapped him on the shoulder and introduced myself, wondering if an apology from me was in order. At first he didn't recognize me, reared away in consternation, then composed himself and leaned forward. "I owe you a thanks. I heard what you said to me in the room that weekend, and it changed me. It was hard to hear, but you were right."

You just never know. Sometimes my greatest accomplishment is keeping my mouth shut; other times my greatest contribution is when I don't.

Match.com

" *ENJOY CANDLELIT DINNERS, WALKS on a moonlit beach, and spending time in the woods enjoying the beautiful nature around us."* Please, spare me. Who writes this cheese? I've perused dating sites and laugh at the liars there. Give me someone who has honed at least *some* self-reflection, won't try to drag my shabby bottom into the woods, and won't assume I'm frothing to participate in the following...

If you want me to scuba dive, skydive, or join you in mountain climbing, or if you are into camping, motorcycles, or any kind of skiing—I may not be the woman for you. Please don't invite me to go horseback riding or play Frisbee with your pit bull. Really. Don't. If you're thinking of dragging me to football, basketball, baseball, boxing, soccer, hockey, wrestling, drag racing, or any loud event where there is a large crowd of Romans, don't bother. And if your life is spent sprawled on the couch in front of the tube glued to such events 24/7, really, really, don't bother. I don't even have a television for godsakes.

If you're an underachiever, unemployed, or looking for someone to take care of you—I've already dated many of you. It won't work out. Trust me.

If you're a right-wing Christian, a rabid Republican, or don't give a rat's patootie about our planet—save yourself from me.

If you have zero self-confidence, have not worked out your stuff with your mother, and live your life to spite your parents, call a therapist.

If you are a drug dealer, a pedophile, or a gang member, call your probation officer.

If you are seriously into pot or a practicing sot, call my ex. You two can chat up one another.

If you have no life, get one. Save your dime. I already have a life and don't need another.

If you are into bondage and whips, multiple partners, or swinging both ways, I'd rather not hear about it, and I don't need pictures either.

If you paint your toenails, spend an hour on your hair, or have head to toe tattoos, hmmm... no.

If you use the words "ya know" or "like" more than twice in a sentence, you'll make me jittery. "Gnarly dude" is also not part of my everyday vocabulary.

If your art display is a collection of beer bottles and baseball caps, I won't be awed.

Herds of dead animals adorning your walls is also a sign we won't be a match made in heaven.

If you're older than my father, forget it. If you're younger than my sons, forget it. I have shoes older than my sons and I don't date men younger than my shoes (mainly because I don't want to explain how old you are to my sons).

So what might we have in common? I dance: swing, country, Cajun, waltz, some ballroom, a little salsa. Most Sunday nights you'll find me on the dance floor, strutting a fast country two-step or whirling the room in a waltz, grinning and dancing cheek to cheek.

A big reader, I also write: I penned a family memoir but then some of my relatives stopped talking to me. My reading tastes tilt toward memoir, fiction, non-fiction, biographies, personal exploration, Enneagram, things like that. (I am a

Self-Preservation One with a Nine wing—which can make me really annoying. Sorry.)

I'm addicted to tracing my family genealogy, not that I *planned* on dead people being my thing.

I just discovered the Marin Farmer's Market, which rocks!

I adore my grandson, whom I date every Thursday and we have ice cream and hang out at the park and go for pizza and talk about important things like sparkle fairies and the new baby.

I love my work, own my business, earn my own money, and find my own way. Eventually.

I like to travel. Well, I like being there, not necessarily getting there. I get dreadfully seasick, tend to get rattled in big cities, and find the wilderness and jungle overrated, but I have journeyed to wondrous places.

Though interested in the world around me, especially people and what makes us tick, I'm not so interested in discussing creation, global warming, or politics if we stand on opposite sides of the fence. These days there appears to be no place for us to meet in the middle. I try not to complain about George Dubya and his current inane and embarrassing administration, as I don't see me doing much about changing it. I don't take a newspaper (I cancelled my subscription, sick to death of reading about Clinton and Monica), and don't care about the latest headlines regarding drunken movie stars, overpaid athletes, and ridiculous reality shows.

I relish good food and dark chocolate. I don't smoke, seldom drink, do swear but try not to when I'm around my brother, did yoga, did meditate, don't go to church, do pray, and practice blessing people who irritate me. I grew up in the 50s and 60s, and am grateful for that. I go to bed when I want and get up when I want. I try to remember that it's none of my business what others think of me—though I do think everyone is entitled to my opinion. I can be on the obsessive-compulsive side, get crabby if I haven't eaten, and have zero sense of direction. My memory left the building with Elvis, so a good part of my time is spent looking for my keys, glasses, and phone; the rest of the time I spend trying to remember what I was going to say. Along with those caveats, I'm healthy, tall, look like I'm in good shape, and have aged well unless it's too early Saturday morning. I'm funny (well, my kids don't think I'm funny, but what do they know), intelligent (though what I don't know I do tend to make up), and generally polite (unless you have crossed me or my Tourette's kicks in.)

But here's the real truth: I am contentedly single, which is why I've not enrolled in online dating. But if I did, this profile is what I'd send to Match.com—just for the heck of it, because from what I've seen, everybody else on there is lying.

2007

WINGNUTS

WE MET AT A HOLIDAY GATHERING. She offered me her hot-pink fake finger-nailed hand, and as an introduction, said, "I'm very spiritual, you know."
I politely responded, "Well are ya, now." I mean, really, how does one follow up on a remark like that without rolling one's eyes? *Whoo whee. This one is gonna be even better than the last two that Bozo fished out of the dating pool.*

After a short exchange, Her Holiness continues, "We haven't been drinking, so we're really looking forward to breaking our fast and celebrating tonight."

Tilting sideways, I snicker, "Then you better fasten your seat belt because I've been here when that river gets flowing."

I sat back and quietly watched as the evening went downhill from there. Sometimes I think I should throw in the towel and drink along with the rest of them. Maybe I'd enjoy the party more, but alcohol makes me throw up. I'd also miss out sitting on the sidelines, judging everyone.

My older son once said, "Mom, others know exactly how you feel about them."

"Good," I responded. "As far as I'm concerned, it saves a lot of time. I don't have to make nice to people I find irritating, and they don't have to suck up to me."

When someone claims to be spiritual, or even better, enlightened, I back away. It's like the minute anyone announces *"you can trust me"* my alarm bells clang. I assume honesty and trustworthiness should be a given, especially in business. I once met an appraiser whose business card read, "Polite, Courteous and Competent." I hadn't looked at his card until after he'd left me on the porch in tears because I couldn't get the key out of the lockbox fast enough to suit him. He refused to come back, putting the timelines in my escrow in jeopardy with a witch of an agent on the other side of the transaction, who'd made it clear she would not give an extension. I was beside myself and the guy was a complete and total jerk.

I love some people's marketing tag lines:

"Integrity You Can Count On"

"A Name You Can Depend On"

"The Most Trusted Name in Real Estate"

The last one is my favorite. Where does that leave the rest of us? Liars? Cheats? Untrustworthy scum? In the pursuit of truth in advertising, I'd put my money on "The Least Trusted Name in Real Estate."

I stopped and thought: uh oh... what's *my* tagline? Of course I couldn't remember. I opened my website and in the upper right hand corner I boldly announce "Moving You in the Right Direction!"

This is from the Realtor with the worst sense of direction in town. However, though I may not have a directional sense in terms of east and west, I'm quite good about directing clients through the maze of real estate, among many other things. So hah.

As I know enough not to trust my directional sense, I also know enough not to trust someone who overtouts their trustworthiness, integrity, or deep spirituality. I realize that not only are they lying to the world, they're fooling themselves, but they don't see that. As humans, we're adept at hiding our shadow side.

I've also learned from experience to distance myself from the complete whack jobs. I know about "fool's trust," which is the foolishness of trusting someone not to do "X" even when they consistently demonstrate they will. If someone is a liar, I trust them to lie. If they cheat, I trust them to cheat. It's like, duh...

I'm aware of my own shadows, so I keep a wary eye on the judgment and contempt in *me*. I attempt to make space for the lamebrains and wingnuts in my life, knowing I too can be lame. When I have space for them to be lame, it gives me space to acknowledge my own ineptness. And when I can't, I roll my eyes and try not to snort tea out my nose.

December 2013

WE JUST WANT
TO BE MAD

M Y SON JON WENT TO THE DOCTOR, as he'd not been feeling well.

"How'd your appointment go, and what did the doctor say? I asked.

"She said I had a cold and could use a psychiatrist."

I laughed.

"Why do you think that's funny?"

"Jon, think about it. With me as your mother, and Bob as your father, why would you think that you *wouldn't* need a psychiatrist? Everyone in this family could use a psychiatrist."

"She also said I had anger issues. Do you think I'm angry?"

I snorted even louder. "Darling, You came into this world infuriated. You were furious as a little kid because you were smaller and being picked on, and you're still furious. You're six-foot-six now, and no one is picking on you any more. You're too tall. It might be time to let some of it go."

"Are you angry?" he asked.

"Yes, but I'm trying to broaden my horizons. Our anger looks different. Yours is overt, mine is covert. Yours is antagonistic, more visible, and shows up as cynicism. Mine leaks out as complaint and resentment, usually because I'm disappointed at what I presume is the unfairness of it all, or that something "shouldn't be." I do have a flash point, but you are more willing to display yours than I am."

We like being angry. In a weird way, it's comforting, like an old slipper. It's also a way to justify our pain. I don't have it that anger is a bad thing, but I try not to wear mine like an Olympic medal. My son and I both hold our anger in our body. If he could whittle his to simply being huffy, and if I could pare mine to just feeling piqued, we'd both be easier to be around—healthier too, not to mention happier.

2014

MEANT TO BE

A T FIRST, IT WAS TO BE JUST THE TWO of them at City Hall. Then it expanded to include our immediate family: the wedding couple, Matt and Brooke and their kids, my sons' father with his girlfriend along with two of his former wives (a family tradition... I'm #1 and Rebecca is #2, but with great disappointment it turned out that #2 was unable to come from Canada; wives #3 and #4 didn't make the guest list).

When I found out what they were planning, and that Jon invited Matt by a text, I asked how they'd feel if I stepped in and interfered. Jon said, "Am I not doing this right?" I said, "Honey, it's not that you're not doing it right, it's just that a wedding is a celebration, an occasion to be witnessed and honored, and I'm not so sure a 41-year-old bachelor—you in particular—should plan his own wedding. And by the by, it's cheesy to text a wedding invitation to your brother." So they let me interfere. The marriage plans were a moving target: who's coming, who can't. Marion's family was unable to as they live in Mississippi and were missed, along with Rebecca (wife #2). It went from possibly Bartholomew Park to my backyard, from no friends to some friends. They were on a budget. They also wanted no cake, flowers, or music, no photographer, spoken vows, or ceremony. I mentioned the wedding might take about twenty seconds with no vows and no ceremony and they said perfect, they didn't like being the center of attention. I also said it might be nice to have a FEW pictures and for them to say SOMETHING to each other and that it was fairly common to have a ceremony, vows, family, friends, food, flowers, a little Champagne, cake, and pictures at a wedding. That's why they call it a wedding and not a hockey game, and we could hang a sheet in front of them if they didn't want anyone to look at them for godsakes.

The event settled into place. When the guest list doubled to twenty, I left a message on Sandra's phone to call me. She and her sister Lynn were doing the food (they owned the Oak Tree Cantina in the late 70s and have known us since Matt and Jon were in grammar school). She called me back and tried to bail as she was only prepared for a small event. I said you can't bail, you're my friend and you've catered weddings before, and you're a fabulous cook, and besides, you made my kids tacos and enchiladas without cheese because they were allergic to dairy when they were young. When the list inched up to twenty-six (Jon was making new friends along the way), I didn't have the courage to inform her in person so I left a mumbling message again on her phone. And I wasn't about to tell her when it hit thirty. I changed the order three times at Wine Country Party for place settings, linen, and chairs, ordered more Champagne, and borrowed patio furniture from Marguerita. Linda talked me off the edge of the cliff when I exhaled that I couldn't seat thirty people in my backyard and she said move the luncheon tables into your living room and food tables to your front room, so we did. With a two-week notice I sent invitations out by *Paperless Post*, which took three nights for me to figure out how it worked. I double-, triple-, and quadruple checked it. I had the right date on the invitation, but managed to have the wrong date on the cover email—of course—so sent a follow-up suggesting folks not come on Thursday as there would be no cake, no Jon, and no Marion on Thursday). Trish worked with me for a week getting the yard ready, Jesus and his brothers came over for four days after their main jobs and turned it into a park.

Phil and Trish helped me set up. Sandra and Lynn didn't quit. They prepared the menu, cooked, delivered, served, and cleaned up. Colleen picked up the tri-tip after Broadway Market forgot to cook it and got it here in plenty of time. Brooke made a fabulous three-tiered naked carrot cake (I know; I never heard of a naked carrot cake either) and greeted the guests with Champagne laced with St. Germaine and raspberries, Matt bartended, Moriah passed hors d'oeuvres and filled in doing whatever was needed, Bob made Satchel happy with a quick card game, Satchel (age 11) stood up for Jon and blessed everyone with a turkey feather, Temple (age 6) was by Marion's side and strew rose petals. Lynn took pictures.

Gary married them with humor, honor, candles, incense, sage, and love. Marion and Jon read their poignant vows, exchanged rings and kissed, I cried, and nobody got drunk. Joe gave a hilarious toast and the house was filled with laughter and happiness. Everything came together perfectly, including the weather.

My favorite parts of the day:
*   When Jon says to me across the luncheon table, "I want to go out back with Marion and have a few more pictures taken." Now this is a man you can't get in front of a camera—not willingly anyway. I look at Matt and Matt looks at me and we look at Jon. "What did you just say?" So Jon says it again and I look back at Matt and Matt looks back at me and with our eyebrows to the sky we ask again, "What did he just say?" And Jon says, "Are you making fun of me?" and we say, "Pretty much... you are a changed man." He says, "I'm growing up," then he and Marion escape for another round of photos.

*   When Gary asks me to sign as witness on the marriage license and I say, "Should I ask Matt to be the second

witness?" and he says, "No, Jon asked his dad." Without the details, this was no small leap on Jon's part. He likes to be mad (it's genetic) and has not been on good terms with Bob for a few years. I'm grateful for yet another healing in the family.

• When Jon and Marion are departing for the weekend and say they have to stop by their house first, and I offer to take their things home for them so they don't get caught in traffic on the way to San Francisco, and Jon says no, "We have to go home for a minute. I want to change my status on Facebook before we leave town."

On May 23, 2014, Jon married the love of his life. We witnessed them standing side-by-side, looking out at the future together. With smiling hearts, we welcomed Marion into the family. I've not seen my son happier or more content.

May 2014

19 NODS TO FACEBOOK

1. Finally! I can quit feeling guilty about not sending Christmas and birthday cards.

2. I'm partial to posts that are interesting, insightful, or just plain weird. Where else would I find a zillion uses for white vinegar, coconut oil, and WD40, or know about the Ellen DeGeneres show.

3. I can leave a comment or an opinion. I can agree or disagree. I can like, or not. And when I think someone is clueless, no one can see my head shaking, though those that know me can hear my eyes rolling.

4. It allows me to practice self-restraint. When I read a post about politics or guns or gays that is really, really retarded, I can't come through the computer to smack anyone upside the head. However, when an occasional post is mean-spirited, out of line, or offensively rude, my fingers become possessed and take over the keyboard. And sometimes I disagree and say so just because I feel like it, though if I'd eaten first I probably could have saved everyone's energy.

5. As far as addictions go, this one is easy on my pocketbook, health, and body. Some days it's a total time suck. However, I like getting a Facebook fix and besides, I'm 65 and can do pretty much whatever I want. My other obsession is genealogy; now THAT'S a time suck, and OMG, talk about being obsessive-compulsive.

6. I'm able to salute birthdays, weddings, births, graduations, retirements, new jobs, new books, new houses, new sweethearts, victory laps, and home runs. I can send blessings to those who have health issues, lost friends and family, or have moved on.

7. I can say hello to relatives and peek in on how folks are doing. I have a huge family and won't be checking in on the majority of them any other way.

8. I know when friends' birthdays are, and feel like a celebrity on mine.

9. It gives me the chance to banter with my sons, who by the by, are both funny.

10. Some posts are profound. Some are wise. Some are hilarious. I cackled at the recent one by the blonde drama queen on Dramamine. My favorite ones are snarky.

11. I can tag along on your vacation and don't have to amble over a month later to sit through three hours of slides. Or have you drag my butt up some mountainside.

12. I get to connect with business friends, dance, writing, and workshop friends, old friends, classmates, kids' friends, friends' kids, long lost friends, and even make new friends.

13. I see who's playing music where and reading poetry when. I find out about recipes, classes, movies, music, books, blogs, events, social media, and things that interest me that I otherwise might have missed. I get to share what calls to me.

14. I love the pictures: old, new, family, friends, yes, *even* some of the dog and cat ones. Just because I'm not an animal person does not make me bad. Seriously, it doesn't. Some of the animal posts are cute, and some of the videos

make me laugh; but the ones billed as: *HILARIOUS! You HAVE to see THIS CAT/DOG/GOAT*—really? The caps are the perfect tip that they are NOT EVEN CLOSE to being hilarious, and shoot me if, like a sucker, I ever open another one that litters my page. Sorry, I went a little sideways here. Where was I?

15. I can hang out with friends and don't have to get dressed, wash my hair, put on make-up, or have them over.

16. I get to share my sweet and rapidly growing grandchildren.

17. It triggers remembrances of the past buried in the corners of my mind.

18. Facebook is a way to be seen and to be heard.

19. It's a way for me to expose my writing with shameless self-promotion. As confident as I am about it, to that same degree I can be insecure. So I appreciate the clapping and huzzahs and "I love your writing!" The support gives me fortitude for the moments when that voice sneaks up behind me and whispers in my ear, "Dearie, your writing sucks."

Side note: I have friends who love my writing and tell me so, often with the encouragement of, "Write on!" When he was four, my son Jon would raise his skinny little arm in the power salute of the day and proclaim, "Right arm!" He was such a goofball... he didn't realize it was "Write on!"

June 2014

None of My Business

RECENT BLOG POST OF MINE provoked a response that mildly caught me by surprise. I sent someone down a rabbit hole regarding my use of the word "retarded" and she nearly tossed me into the briar patch when I read her response. But hey, at least I'm being read and she took the time to comment. In case you missed it:

19 Nods to Facebook (previous story):

#4. It allows me to practice self-restraint. When I read a post about politics or guns or gays that is really, really retarded, I can't come through the computer to choke them.

A bird of a feather reposted my **19 Nods** on her Facebook page, and here are the comments that followed:

My friend Catherine, your writing makes me laugh. Not the "funny-picture" kind of laugh, but the "funny-view-of-life" kind of laugh. So I post your humor. And say... thanks.

Me: I so appreciate the repost as it gets my musings to a larger audience. You are a peach!

Her friend Apart from the insensitive use of the "R" word in #4, I love the list. For only that reason, I can't repost. These make me feel justified in spending fb time!

My friend referencing a dictionary: **re·tard·ed**
Adjective:
~less advanced in mental, physical, or social development than is usual for one's age
~informal offensive
~very foolish or stupid
~"in retrospect, it was a totally retarded idea"

Her friend Do the decent thing and use a word that doesn't insult people with disability, demean them and pain those who love them.

My friend I appreciate your comment. And, I also know that words morph into meaning things different than when they started. Including morphing into insults (when they initially weren't insults). Certainly, the initial definition doesn't suggest an insult. Your comment is a reminder that words are powerful and do have an impact. Glad you enjoyed the rest of the post!

I mulled over this conversation, attempting to sort out how it struck me, then emailed three writer compatriots for their take:

Writer friend #1 Hmmm! I guess the word didn't land on me. It went right by, Catherine. At one level I guess we all have to decide when we write and put it out there if we can tolerate disapproval from some people. How much approval do I need? Then, is some of the impact of others back on us worth considering in our own evolution? I totally get you don't want to Windex and squeegee all your words. All the color that is yours would be gone.

Writer friend #2 Well, we know there is no meaning in reality, only what we bring to it. That said, I find the insult to having had that word applied to the disabled in the first place. But I like the word. The definition applies and qualifies in many situations. Politicians come to mind. Bigots come to mind. Ideas come to mind. Yes, we throw it around too freely, but a developmentally disabled person is not what I picture when I use it. Others will, but that's their problem. I think the bottom line is, how are you meaning it and does it describe best what you are trying to get across. We can always find a better way to say something, but as you say, do we have to go around worrying about offending everyone's petty sensibilities? Now THAT'S retarded.

Cindy Catherine, I can only offer my opinion, which you can freely ignore. What good Leo doesn't love to get advice and then toss it? Technically the word "retarded" shouldn't have connotations. It ought to mean just what the dictionary says. But it's an avoid word. So I avoid it and other perfectly good words even as I mourn the loss of their rightful place in our language. But I will also support your choice if you wish to stand firm and use it!

The line from the objector that caught my attention was: "do the *decent* thing," as if I'd done something *indecent*. Ahh, the things that trip us up from our past. I have an early incident with my mother (I'd gone to live with her when I was five, and the first words I remember her speaking to me were: "Sit here and be quiet, be good, and don't touch anything.") The feelings of that long ago event resurfaced in me, pricking me where I am, you might say, a bit thin-skinned: *I must be in trouble, I'd better behave.* It also triggered my usual response: *How did I get here? I didn't do anything wrong.* This was yet another rerun of my very own movie.

I appreciated the opportunity to give all this some thought, because once my book is published and I have a wider audience than family and friends (though that may be magical thinking on my part), the naysayers of the world will stream out of the woodwork; it comes with the territory. Not everyone is going to appreciate my writing or my humor, and if they take umbrage, that's their stuff. It's none of my business what they think of me, or my work. (Now, this is easy to say, not so easy to do...). My writer friend #2 would counsel me: "Buck up, baby, quit worrying what others think."

As one who banters with humor, sarcasm, and bluntness, I'm not always politically correct, and it surfaces in my tirades and asides. Sometimes it gets me in trouble. I'm used to getting flak from family. My brother gets on me about swearing, and out of deference, I curb my language, though I have pointed out to him that "puke" and "snot" are not swear words and to please quit crossing them out. On occasion, socially obnoxious words do sneak into my sentences under the cover of dark.

Compared to the majority of online criticisms I see, the woman who got her panties in a bunch was mild and well-meaning, and nothing compared to my sister who threatened to put a hex on me regarding a story I wrote about her in my family memoir. I'm still ricocheting from that one. If I'm able to touch another enough to inspire them, move them to laugh or cry, have them ponder something beyond their linty navel, snap them out of their stupor, or heaven forbid—piss them off—then perhaps I'll have made a difference. Isn't that the point? And if it goes a step further and we have an interaction, positive or otherwise, at least I'll know I'm not yammering away to the walking dead. The only way writers know they are being read is when someone yammers back.

July 2014

SHAKEN, NOT STIRRED

PRELUDE: AUGUST 22, 2014

My birthday was last week but I had the flu. Matt and Brooke planned a party for me for tonight (dinner at Breakaway, cake, Stompers baseball game), but I still have the flu (which they gave me by the by).

"You're going to have my party without me?" I wailed.

Matt said, "Why not? We have the tickets and the dinner plans, so we're still going to all go (Matt, Brooke, the kids, Jon and Marion).

I said, "What about my cake?"

He said, "Don't worry, we'll eat your cake too."

The brats better not open my presents. Wait a minute, they probably didn't even get me any presents... I want a redo.

All right already, so it takes an earthquake to get me out of bed. After ten days nursing the flu, I wake up to my house rolling one way, then rocking the other. The earth is jolting and roaring. My bedroom is upstairs where there is extra sway. The door to my upper deck has blown open and I see transformers are exploding in the neighborhood, filling my room with an eerie blue light. Pictures, candelabras, and vases are falling off the mantel and shelves, crashing onto furniture and the brick hearth, pottery breaking and glass shattering. I think: aren't you supposed to get out of bed and lie right next to it on the floor during an earthquake? And then I think: screw that, I have an angel framed mirror that weighs a ton right next to me that could take me out, or an eight-foot armoire that could tumble and kill me. If I'm going to die, it's going to be in my bed hiding under my down comforter between soft white sheets. I want to be comfortable when my time comes.

It lasts nearly a minute, which is an eternity, especially with everything in slow motion, but it gives me time to be grateful that I don't live in the Middle East, that it's not a bomb, and that I'm on the upper level in case my house has a mind to collapse. Then it stops, and it's now eerily quiet. This may be the most rattled I've ever been. I didn't think I was going to die, but I also thought my house could well come tumbling down. Feeling my way in the dark, naked and barefoot, I close the door to my deck, just missing the glass shards all over the floor. I find my cell phone to see what time it is: 3:23 a.m. I crawl back into bed and text my kids and friends to see if they're okay. I can't email on my phone—well, I probably could if I could figure out how to set it up—but it dawns on me I can get Facebook. It was comforting. I didn't feel like I was by myself; everyone on there was all right and checking in with each other. I could also get the news: it was a 6.0 between Napa and American Canyon, power outages, roads closed, the strongest earthquake in this area in 25 years. Facebook is amazing in an emergency.

By morning my phone battery was nearly dead. My power was out so I tried charging it in my car without the engine on. Supposedly that works in some cases. Not in mine. I thought about turning on the engine but I couldn't open the automatic garage door. There's this red cord I could pull, but then I was afraid I couldn't close it. And if I ran the engine in the closed garage, people might have thought I'd killed myself on purpose because my older son went ahead and had my birthday party without me two days ago, and my younger son forgot my birthday altogether and didn't return my text or phone call when I checked to see if he and his wife were okay. When I tried him again about 10:00, Jon was driving around trying to find coffee and something for breakfast. I asked out of curiosity if it had occurred to him to check to see if I was all right. He said no, actually, it hadn't. I didn't bother to tell him I'd also noticed he hadn't called to see how I was or if I needed anything while I was sick. I suppose, because we live less than a mile away from one another, that would be superfluous. I knew Matt and his family were okay because Brooke texted me back. I should have had girls.

Were these boys raised by wolves? Were they carried by crackhead mothers and switched on me at birth in the hospital? Or are they simply brain dead? That must be it. Which means it's my fault. I shouldn't have dropped acid in the 60s. It genetically damaged both of them.

Most of us in Sonoma were lucky. Some had more damage than others, but apparently nothing major. I'm grateful that we are all safe and no one was hurt; compared to so many of the major earthquakes occurring all over the world, this one was no great shakes. Besides, we need a good shaking once in a while to remind us how precious our time on this earth is. This one caught my attention.

I posted the above on Facebook the day of the earthquake, August 24, 2014, and here are the responses:

Matt Sevenau (my son) Was there an earthquake last night? Nice to know you're feeling better. Must be that $80 chocolate birthday cake that fixed you all up. We will find a nice home for you when the time comes, as Alzheimer's seems to be setting in rapidly for you.
August 24 at 4:48pm

Karen Love this Cathy, and Matthew behave yourself and go over to your Mothers and give her a piece of her birthday cake. The least you could do!!!!!
August 24 at 4:48pm

Catherine Sevenau He did bring me cake. He didn't bring me any dinner, but he did bring me cake, handing it out the car window on the way to the game. I've been sick in bed for over a week, why would he think I'd be hungry? Maybe he thinks I live on air and light alone. Maybe he thinks fish and loaves miraculously appear in my refrigerator. Maybe he's an idiot.
August 24 at 4:50pm

Matt Sevenau Already hand delivered Karen, on Friday night. She ate the whole thing and now the caffeine is taking over.
August 24 at 4:50pm

Shawnda My son #1 (27yo): He texted at 10:15: "did you guys feel that?" I call him back - I'm 10 seconds into describing the horror and he says "um, can I call you back - I'm busy right now." My son #2 (26yo): I texted early this morning to say: "if you hear about an earthquake up here, just want you to know we're ok." He called at 1:39 pm. My son #3 (15yo): slept through the whole thing. So, I think you need to have another son. After all, 3 is the magic number.
August 24 at 4:50pm

Catherine Sevenau Three boys??? I'd have to hang myself.
August 24 at 4:53pm

Matt Sevenau Better than 5 moms!!!
August 24 at 4:53pm

Catherine Sevenau That's your father's doing, not mine.
August 24 at 4:54pm

Matt Sevenau Glad all is well with your home mom. We could use a little help around here cleaning up if you're not too busy.
Matt posts a photo of a house completely collapsed (not his).
August 24 at 5:10pm

Catherine Sevenau Yikes, is this in Sonoma?
August 24 at 5:10pm

Matt Sevenau My house. Thanks for checking in...
August 24 at 5:11pm

Catherine Sevenau Oh quit trying to make my friends feel sorry for you; it is pathetic. You really should have brought me dinner on my birthday you know.
August 24 at 5:13pm

Matt Sevenau They were my friends first!
August 24 at 5:14pm

Catherine Sevenau Not any more...
August 24 at 5:16pm

Matt Sevenau Just a couple more bricks to go and I think I'll get the kids out okay. Don't fret we will be fine.
Matt posts a second photo (in Napa), of a whole block completely demolished.
August 24 at 5:16pm

Catherine Sevenau OMG, you ARE pathetic.
August 24 at 5:17pm

Jerry This is too funny!!
August 24 at 5:30pm

Sheila Very funny!
August 24 at 5:51pm

Catherine Clemens Sevenau There's a lot more I could write, but they'd come after me.
August 24 at 5:55pm

Matt Sevenau They won't come after you. Sonoma Developmental Center is not adding new patients.
August 24 at 5:57pm

Catherine Sevenau Jon always said he'd put me in a GOOD home. And I wasn't referring to the royal "they." I was referring to my family, of which you were once a part.
August 24 at 5:58pm

Tina I love you Catherine Sevenau!!! Happy belated, glad ur alright and glad ur recovering from ur flu. I always enjoy reading ur writing. See u this week. Xoxo
August 24 at 6:03pm

Lynn My oldest daughter keeps telling me I can go live with my youngest daughter in New York... high end Long Island - btw - in her basement with the door locked. Don't you love how our kids are so concerned and caring?
August 24 at 6:30pm

Catherine Sevenau brats, I say, goddam little brats
August 24 at 6:31pm

Lynn What worries me most is that we raised them... wtf???
August 24 at 6:32pm

Melissa Matt Sevenau, too funny. Jon Sevenau, staying silent... there is wisdom in that. Love you all. Happy belated birthday, glad you are feeling better.
August 24 at 7:04pm

Matt Sevenau Update: my children just got pulled out of the rubble and both will most likely live. Son Satchel just came out of coma and asked how his Oma fared. I let him know that

I think she will be okay once she gets the artwork on walls straightened out.
August 24 at 7:12pm

Elaine Too funny!
August 24 at 7:17pm

Catherine Sevenau Don't encourage him. At least my grandson asked about me.
August 24 at 7:17pm

Paul Ah, life in the Napa Valley.
August 24 at 7:17pm

Catherine Sevenau We live in the Sonoma Valley you dingdong.
August 24 at 7:18pm

Leslie Funny and so true about the texting Moms. My sympathy and it's shared, now I know I'm not alone. Thank you Catherine for the wonderful story!
August 24 at 7:18pm

Matt Sevenau Six injured in Napa and only one injured in Sonoma. I do believe Catherine is now in stable condition and all is well for today.
August 24 at 7:26pm

Catherine Sevenau Actually, I just cut the crap out of my finger dumping glass. My grandchildren will love the war wound. My children won't care.
August 24 at 7:28pm

Matt Sevenau Proof!
Matt posts a screen shot of my "are you okay" text
August 24 at 7:33pm

Catherine Sevenau Proof schmoof. I don't see your name anywhere on this text, other than me addressing you at the very top. Brooke is who responded to my, "You okay?" I like her way better than you. She is also the one that took care of arranging my birthday party (you know, the one you had without me) and ordering the cake. However, yes, you did hand it to me out the window of your car as you drove by on your way to the game. I've had it for dinner, breakfast and lunch. I should eat something else before I go into a diabetic coma.
August 24 at 7:42pm

Matt Sevenau That was me texting you on her phone since she was on mine calling 911. Once we knew you were safe we could then dig for children.
August 24 at 7:45pm

Catherine Sevenau You are going to hell you know.
August 24 at 7:46pm

Laura Shame on you Matt Sevenau and Jon Sevenau - you need to check on your mother!!! Glad you're ok Cath!
August 24 at 7:48pm

Marsha LOL!!! Catherine, you have an interesting, and I'm sure challenging, family! I thought mine was odd... you win!
August 24 at 7:54pm

Catherine Sevenau You have no idea, no idea...
August 24 at 7:54pm

Matt Sevenau Late morning phone call follow up after early morning text. Just ordered lifetime supply of gingko biloba for next year's birthday present.
Matt posts a screen shot of his phone proving he called me.
August 24 at 7:55pm

Catherine Sevenau I never said you didn't call me, I said your brother didn't call me. Besides, you didn't call to see how I was; you called because you had a question about real estate. Now leave me alone. I notice he hasn't chimed in on either this thread or my party thread. Smart boy.
August 24 at 7:57pm

Judy HAHAHAHAH. PEED AGAIN!! you guys killin me. Cath, once I was at the farmers market with heat stroke. I called my son John and said YOU HAVE TO COME DOWN HERE AND HELP ME. IM GOING TO PASS OUT. He says, "who is this?" I give up!! Gotta love em! Who else would!!
August 24 at 7:57pm

Catherine Sevenau Their wives.
August 24 at 7:57pm

Judy Blame it on their dad, works every time. Haha
August 24 at 8:02pm

Catherine Sevenau Oh, you mean the one with the five wives? That would be too easy.
August 24 at 8:02pm

Patricia That's the way boys are... your story was a great read.
August 24 at 8:17pm

Irene Yep... sounds like you should have had girls!! Happy you are all safe. Do you remember the earthquake in 1968-69. Scary... but you make it through.
August 24 at 8:36pm

Catherine Sevenau Yes, It was in early October of 1969. I was six months pregnant with Matt, living on St. Helena Avenue in Santa Rosa. It threw me from the bathroom into the

living room. Maybe that's what's wrong with him. Bob worked for Safeway in Sonoma at the time.
August 24 at 8:38pm

Matt Sevenau Ahhh, the summer of love...
August 24 at 8:59pm

Julie I'm still laughing... at least you raised him to be funny.
August 24 at 9:35pm

Susan The exploding transformers were the highlight of the show, let's not do that again for another 20 years!
August 24 at 10:22pm

Becca I'll be first in line for the Sevenau Comedy Hour on KSVY! You guys are good--sharp, funny, quick. And Catherine Clemens Sevenau, we mothers are with you, still waiting for that text . . .
August 25 at 8:18am

August 2014

HEARING EGGS

A FEW MONTHS AGO it was my eyes. As I could no longer see to drive at night, I had my vision checked. The doctor said my cataracts were so bad that he was surprised I could see during the day. So I had both eyes "done" and I can see clearly now: stars, leaves, street signs, menus, wrinkles, my grandchildren's new teeth. It's an amazingly colorful world out there that had gone gray without me noticing.

Yesterday I had my hearing checked (I thought I heard just fine; I'd received a birthday card from a local hearing aid company in the mail with a $25 gift certificate and figured if someone wanted to give me $25, I was in, and while I was there, they could check my ears.) After testing, I was told I had 50% hearing loss, and that I needed hearing eggs.

I said, "WHAT?" So I paid attention, and she was correct, I couldn't hear half of what was going on.

Last week at an MLS real estate meeting, before I found out I was half deaf, I was making an announcement on the microphone. Felice, who was sitting across the room, shouts out, "Nice hair." Before she came into real estate she owned a hair salon and did my hair and cut the boys'.

I put the microphone closer to my mouth and said, "Can you hear me now?"

She says, "I said, 'nice hair.'"

I reposition the mic and say, "Now can you hear me?" The whole room is laughing except me.

"I can HEAR you fine. I said I liked your HAIR."

"Oh, thanks," and then I do a shout out for Kristin, who I've been going to for the past twenty-some years.

At the next week's meeting I stood up with the microphone to make another announcement and opened up with, "How's my hair?" which is now a running joke in the room.

Linda, my business partner, had noticed my hearing loss for some time; she said I was forever asking people to repeat themselves or turn up the volume. Funny how we miss that we're going blind and deaf. My health insurance covered my eye surgery, but does not cover hearing eggs. We'll see how long I can go using the ones out of my refrigerator. I think you have to poke a hole in each end and blow them out for them to work. In the meantime, I'd appreciate it if you could speak up a little.

Since we're talking about hearing eggs...

I was in the back seat with my friend Kayla, who was three at the time (she just turned eighteen), and we were on the way to Wally and PJ's for Easter. Ed and Elaina (her grandparents, who were raising her) are in front.

Kayla shows me her Easter basket and announces, "I got eggs."

I say, "No, you have eggs."

She says, "I know, I just said that."

I say, "Look, it's not, I 'got' eggs, it's I 'have' eggs."

She says, "You don't got eggs. I got eggs."

Ed says, "Uh oh, I can tell this is going to be a long ride."

I say, "Kayla, this isn't a possession conversation, it's a grammar conversation."

Ed, rolling his eyes in the rearview mirror, chimes in, "Great, that clears it right up for a three-year-old."

She hugs her basket tightly to her chest and says, "They're mine!"

I ignore him and continue... "Darling, I know they're yours and I'm not taking them, I promise, but when you have eggs in your basket you don't say: I 'got' eggs, you say: I 'have' eggs."

At that point we arrive, and as we climb out of the car Kayla looks up at me, shows me her collection and says proudly, "I have eggs."

I rest my hand on the top of her head and beam at her freckled little face, "You certainly do!"

And that's how you teach grammar to a smart three-year-old.

P.S. Over the years, we've signed our cards to each other with, "p.s. I have eggs."

P.P.S. As Kayla has eggs, and since she's an artist, she can make me a headband with two brown eggs with the yolks blown out glued to the bottom of each side positioning them near my ears. It will look like a headset, and if she dyes them red, they'll match my hair.

4.

SMALL FRY
REVERIES

Ancient Being

I HELD MY GRANDSON for the first time shortly after his birth. I remember having this tiny being cradled in my arms, peering into his dark eyes, thinking he looked nothing like a baby, but rather like a wise and ancient being.

A week later I went to see him again and brought Marie, my stepmother. We were at Matt and Brooke's house, and as Marie, 85, was the matriarch and elder in the family, I offered to have her hold Satchel first. Twenty minutes passed, and I was itching to have him.

"Can I hold him now?'

"No," she said, "I still want him."

"I'd like to hold him."

She again refused my request.

"It's my turn."

"No."

"You mean you're not going to let me hold my grandson?"

"When I'm done," she said coolly.

Something in me snapped and I leaned forward, latched onto his little foot, and barked, "Give me that baby!"

"No!"

By now I'm actually yanking on his leg. She won't let go, and I'm trying to snatch him from her. My son, watching this tug-of-war, snorts, "Oh my God, somebody get me a video camera."

Realizing that I now appear crazed, I let go. She reluctantly handed him over to me, as she knew I was coming after her next.

I'll never be the wise woman in the family, not as long as anyone comes between that child and me.

March 2003

THE WHITE ANGEL

W E WERE AT THE SONOMA VALLEY Museum of Art for "The Day of the Dead" exhibition. Satchel was less than a year old and I had him on my hip, carrying him around to look at the fascinating exhibits decorated with personal photos, candles, and marigolds. We stood entranced before a magnificent ten-foot angel resplendent in a long white gown with elegant wings and a halo of blonde hair.

My grandson sucked in his breath, then released it with a soft, "Pretty."

I was stunned that a nine-month-old child understood the concept of pretty. It was also the first word that he spoke with me.

November 2004

A COLONY OF BEES

SATCHEL WAS MAYBE TWO, and we were holding hands crossing Broadway, walking from my office to the park. I heard their eerie sound before I saw them. We were in front of the first car in the intersection, and out of nowhere, not six feet away, also in the intersection and heading straight into us, was a huge swarm of honeybees.

I grabbed Satchel by his skinny little arm, and backpedalled in what seemed like slow motion to get out of their path. Then everything sped up to warp speed as we made it under the corner bank's overhang, squatting together, my body shielding his. My grandson had on a tank top, shorts, and sandals, and though I had less skin exposed, I'm allergic to bees.

"Oma, that was close! What WAS that?"

"Darling, that was our life passing before our eyes."

As the swarm continued up the street, I explained it was a colony of bees, probably from one of the trees in the park looking for a new home, and that we were lucky we got out of their way. He had no idea how lucky.

My first memory was being stung by a bee, and it could very well have been my last.

2005

MELTDOWN

MY GRANDSON IS THREE and I have him for the day. Brooke and Matt are in San Francisco, returning late, around 10:00 p.m.

We spend the afternoon and evening at my house doing all the things we love to do together: cooking, eating, and reading the books I read to his father and Uncle Jon when they were his age. I taught Satchel to make scrambled eggs, which is now his specialty.

Getting him into his dragon pajamas, I tell him it's time for me to take him home.

"NOOOO! I want to stay here!"

"C'mon. I'm supposed to have you home and in bed in an hour." He throws himself on the floor, kicking and screaming, apparently possessed. I'm taken by surprise, as he's such an even-keeled little guy. I scoop him up and head downstairs. Having turned into a writhing demon and trying to escape from my arms, he nearly throws us both down the staircase.

When we get to the bottom he hurls himself to the floor, completely out of control.

"Satchel, get up and stop it."

His screaming escalates. I give fair warning. "If you don't stop, I'm going to smack your bottom." What I really want to do is take a fire hose and blast him, but I don't have one handy.

"Okay, I warned you." I lift him up by his skinny little arm and give him a swat on the butt. He's so shocked that he stops, then proceeds into a meltdown of uncontrollable tears, sobbing and shaking, far beyond the point of turning it around.

After some minutes of this, I bargain with him: "Look, if I take you to Busha's (his other grandmother) will you quit crying?" He nods between sobs. Of course I don't have her number and only vaguely know where she lives. He assures me he can find her house. We circle her neighborhood three times while he hiccoughs through sobs in the back seat.

He poses, "Mmmm. Turn here." Then, "Mmm, turn here."

He has no idea how to get there either. I realize this when he wants me to cross the highway to Boyes Boulevard. Why do I trust the directions of a three-year-old? As I drive past my friend Rhonda's house, I think maybe a third person can snap him out of this. She's home and answers our knock.

We pick figs and pears and slice them up on her back porch. Then she brings out a box of magic toys and Satchel and I put on matching red noses. She takes our picture, noting we look quite a lot alike. Satch has calmed down, though he's still not himself.

It is well past sunset by the time I deliver him to his house, but as I try to put him to bed, the tears and wracking sobs return. For the next hour and a half I sit on the front porch steps in the dark, rocking him back and forth, his sobs continuing through his drift toward sleep.

When Matt and Brooke come home, I tell them how the evening went.

Matt calls the next day, not happy with me. "We don't spank him, you know."

"I've noticed."

"Did you spank us when we were kids?"

"Apparently not enough," I respond.

"You did too, you spanked us with the wooden spoon!"

"I did not, I chased you with the wooden spoon; you were both faster than me. I did not spank you, and Aunt Liz was the first one to spank Jon, an event he's still not recovered from. I did wale on him a couple of times after that, however. Look Matt, I want to honor how you raise your child. But I'm telling you, if he ever pulls that with me again, you're coming to get him, I don't care where you are. And by the by, just what *do* you suggest I should have done?"

"Well, we put him in his bedroom and hold the door knob so he can't get out."

"Great, that would be unsafe to do in *any* room in my house, and would go over *real* big at my office."

I don't see Satchel for a couple of weeks. Supposedly he is still mad at me, but I'm pretty sure kids don't hang onto things that long. Small kids, anyway. Two weeks later we're at the park and I'm pushing him in the swing.

He asks tentatively, "Oma, can we go to your house?"

"Forget it. Last time we were at my house, you got upset and I got in trouble. We're staying right here on neutral ground."

Looking up with the same brown eyes his father had when he was little, my grandson says in a quiet voice, "Then maybe can we go next week?"

"We can go next week—on one condition. When I ask you to do something, you don't throw a hissy fit when you don't get your way. Deal?"

"Deal!" he promises.

2006

TELEVISION

"OMA, YOU DON'T HAVE A TELEVISION," Satchel says to me in surprise.

"You've known me for four years, and you've just noticed?"

"Why don't you like TV?"

"I didn't say I didn't like TV, I just don't have one."

"Did you ever?"

"Of course. I had one when your dad and Jon were growing up, but when they both moved away to college, I let your dad take it to school."

"Didn't he get in trouble with his teacher?"

"No, he wasn't going to a Waldorf college," I say, trying not to laugh. "He didn't take it to his classroom. He was twenty years old and brought it to the house he lived in. It was for him and his roommates."

I can see his little wheels spinning. "So, Oma. IF you had a TV, where would you put it?" He takes my hand and leads me to face the logical spot over the fireplace. "You could put it there!"

"That will never do. First of all, it will wreck my decor, and secondly, why do I want a television set?"

My grandson looks up at me with his soft brown eyes and says dreamily, "For me."

"Darling, I'm not getting a TV, not even for you. Pick out a book and I'll read you a story instead."

2007

164

BAT WINGS

“**O**MA, WHY DOES THE SKIN HANG DOWN on your arm like that?”

“What!”

“Why does the skin hang down on your arm like that?”

My grandson is commenting on my underarms from his car seat in the back as we’re driving down East Napa Street. I’m trying to fathom why a four-year-old boy would notice such a thing in the first place, much less comment on it.

“I heard you the first time,” I retorted. “I’m getting older, and not in shape like I once was.”

“Exercise would take care of that, you know.”

“WHAT?”

The only time I’d ever been in a gym was to pick him up from daycare while his mother was at spin class. I laughed when I saw what a spin class was. I had visions of everyone sitting in colored plastic snow tubs spinning around, which would only make me sick. I didn’t get the point. When I saw what it really was, I still didn’t get the point. Why not just ride a bicycle, for Pete’s sake.

A week later, on the same road, he asks me the same question.

“Tell me again why your arms hang down like that?”

I think: *this kid must have a death wish.*

“Look, Satchel, we’ve had this conversation. Just for the record, I have no intention on going to a gym. Or exercising. Or lifting weights. I’ve watched people exercise every day of their lives, and they ended up dead anyway. Besides, I know how to resolve this. From here on out, I'm wearing long sleeved shirts."

2007

Dead People and Sparkle Fairies

"**O**MA, THERE'S DEAD PEOPLE under those rocks, you know."

I glance over my shoulder to see what Satchel is talking about. My four-year-old grandson is commenting from his car seat about the small cemetery to our left on East Napa.

"I know Satchel, that's where they put our bodies when we die."

"What do they do with the heads?" he asks.

"Well, when we die we don't need our bodies any more," I elaborate further with a spiritual conversation about bodies and souls and death.

When I finish, he says, "Yeah, but what do they do with *the heads?*"

As I attempt to expound further, he interrupts and gasps, "Oma! The car is filled with sparkle fairies!"

I'm wearing a Brazilian rhinestone bracelet my sister Liz gave me, and the sun is bouncing off the facets, sprinkling the car's interior with hundreds of tiny brilliant refractions.

He asks in wonder, "Can you see them?"

"I can, Satchel, that I can."

Then he tilts his head forward and says, "Oma, can you see the Apple Fairy on the top of my head?"

I peer in the rearview mirror, slip into his world of magic, and tell him, "Of course. How long has she been there?"

"About a week!"

"A week! That's amazing. You are certainly a lucky boy, Satchel."

A few days later, I was telling my friend Elaina the cemetery story. I hadn't understood his question until she laughed and said, "Well, you told him what they did with the *bodies*. He wanted to know what they did with the *heads*."

I didn't get back to him on that one. By then we'd moved on to Sparkle Fairies and the Apple Fairy and Hitler and bad men, and it all seemed too much to have to reopen the death conversation. He's under the assumption that their dog Sam and his great-grandpa Calvin are on the roof because everyone looks up and points to heaven when he asks what happened to them.

2007

HITLER WAS
A BAD MAN

MATT TOOK SATCHEL to Mountain Cemetery on Memorial Day to honor Satchel's deceased great-grandfather Calvin Frost, and dropped him off afterwards to spend the day with me.

In great excitement Satchel bursts through the front door. "Oma! Oma! Did you know that Grandpa Cal fought in the war and won all the battles and at the end of the war he killed Hitler?"

"Do tell. I think you got most of the story right."

"What?" he asks, stopping short.

"Well, Grandpa Cal did fight in the war, and he may have won all the battles, but at the end of the war he didn't kill Hitler."

"Who did?"

"Hitler was the leader of Germany and a very bad man. When the Allied Forces invaded his country, he knew he'd lost the war and would be taken prisoner, so he killed himself."

"Oh." He lets this sink in, then asks, "Do you have any pictures of Hitler?"

"Not hanging on my walls, but I suppose we could find what he looks like on the computer."

After some time on the Internet, he's satisfied and says, "Oma, you were right. Hitler was a *very* bad man." He thinks a bit, then says, "Do we have any bad men in the family?"

"No, but we have someone in the family who was killed by a bad man."

"Who!"

"Harry Tracy was a very bad man in the Wild West, and he shot Valentine Hoy, my great-grandmother's brother."

"Do you have any pictures of *him*?"

"Well, as a matter of fact, I do." I pull out my book of Hoy history and show Satchel the pictures of Harry and Valentine.

He asks, leafing through it, "Oma, what is this?"

"It's a book Uncle Gordon and I put together about our family history. This one is on my mother's side of the family, and it's about her, and her parents, and their parents, and all of their families on our Hoy side, from the time they left Germany and came to this country."

"Is my mom's family in here?"

"No, it's your dad's side of the family."

He turns the pages, interested in everything.

"Would you like a copy of it when you grow up?" I ask.

"I would," he says, oh so earnestly.

"I knew I liked you," and I kiss the top of his four-year-old head.

The next day I get a call from his father. "Is there any *particular* reason you're having a conversation with my son about Hitler?"

To that I respond, "Hey, you're the one that opened it up. I didn't bring him to the cemetery, you did. I was simply answering his questions."

November 2007

JUST A SAYING

A S I'M GETTING LUNCH TOGETHER, Satchel is on my kitchen floor with both legs encircling my ankle, his arms around my calf. When I try to walk away, he hangs on, hoping for a ride. I'm wearing black cowboy boots.

I lose my balance and bark, "Watch out! If I come down on you with my heel, you won't be having any children."

"What do you mean, I won't be having any children?"

"If I crush your cojones, you won't be able to have kids."

"What do you mean, I won't be able to have kids?"

Ohmygod. I've had the death conversation. I've had the Hitler conversation. And now I'm heading into the sex conversation with a four-year-old?

I stutter and stammer. "It's just, well, it's just, it's just, it's just a... " grasping for words.

He saves me. "Oh, you mean, it's just a saying?"

"Exactly, it's just a saying." I exhale with relief. I've already been in enough trouble this month answering his questions.

November 2007

Dragons

ROOKE AND THE KIDS ARE VISITING in Sonoma for a month. My son and his family relocated to Vancouver, Canada, in August of last year. They had the nerve not only to move there, but also to take my grandchildren with them, and this is their first time back. Satchel is six but tall enough to look like eight. We do our favorite things: cook eggs (he scrambles), play dominoes (he wins), draw dragon pictures (he makes good castles, I make good trees), bake chocolate chip cookies (he does it all, "let me, let me," other than cracking open the eggs as eggshells in batter are a drag), and eat out (his favorite restaurant: The Red Grape).

Last week we had lunch there. Pemba greets us at the door. He remembers Satchel and is pleased to see him again. They make small talk, he seats us, then comes back to take our order. "What would she like?" Pemba asks. I stick my head behind the menu, lean in and whisper, "He." Flustered, Pemba apologizes to Satchel and says he'd gotten confused and had *thought* he was a boy, and...

Satchel says "That's okay," and as Pemba walks away, my grandson mutters, "that is *sooo* irritating."

"Well, you can see how people get confused. Why do you think that is?"

"My hair," he says, which is now down to the middle of his skinny little back.

"Well, what could you do about it?"

"I could cut it."

"And when do you think that might be?"

"When I'm ten."

"So then here's the deal: upon occasion for the next four years, you get to be irritated."

We play tic-tac-toe (he wins) until our order comes.

July 2009

PINK SPARKLES

MY GRANDDAUGHTER IS A YEAR and three months, all pink and sparkles. She waves frantically hello as if she's truly happy to see you, and kisses you sweetly goodbye as if she truly loves you. I think both are true. New at walking, she careens like a drunken sailor and every fifteen minutes like a clock pinging the quarter hour, cracks her head on something, howls for nine seconds, and is up and staggering again, exploring her two-and-a-half-foot-high world on the run.

Temple adores her brother and is as cute as cute can be, but is no shrinking violet. Satchel gets in her face, and when she's had enough, she lets out a banshee wail and latches onto his cheek or arm like a five-clawed lobster, digging her adorable little painted fingernails right in. She did it to me once and I see why he stops bugging her. It's brutal, and no, I wasn't teasing her. I think she was just letting me know for future reference who might be in charge—if the question were to arise.

Between the head nodding, signing (quickly tapping her fingertips together for "more"), and a vocabulary sufficient to get one through any domestic area or foreign country, she communicates succinctly and clearly.

She finally has hair, soft tufts of blonde. Her mother cut it so you could see her little neck. Wrong head. I now have one grandchild who is mistaken for a girl and the other who could be taken for a boy.

They head back to Canada in a few days. Their poppa misses them terribly. I know how he feels.   *July 2009*

Looking Good

D URING A BIRTHDAY PARTY FOR BROOKE, I sat in the corner hanging out with all the little kids. They were each piping up with how old they were when Satchel reaches up and pats me on the head and beams, "My Oma is 62, but she looks really good for her age. She could pass for 60!"

November 2010

Meltdown
Postscript

"**O**MA, I REMEMBER when you spanked me."
"Good. As far as I can tell, it worked out great."
"It hurt, you know."
"Oh for godsakes, Satchel, that was five years ago, you had on diapers, and it was one well-placed swat. And it wasn't like I was punishing you; I was trying to snap you out of a meltdown. The only thing I hurt, Cupcake, was your feelings, and I think you've recovered by now."

2011

THE BOY AND THE GIRL

WHEN HE WAS LITTLE, Satchel was all fun, fun, fun. "Can we go to the movies and to the toy store and bake cookies and play dominoes and can you read me a book and then go to the park can we huh? huh?

I ask, "All in the next three hours?

He says, "Sure!"

He takes after his father.

He has a sister now, Temple, who dresses herself, and is all girl. She's usually in head-to-toe pink, wearing a glittery top with a tutu, matching tights, and sparkly shoes.

She takes after her mother.

I have them once or twice a week and it only takes me a day or two to recover. Mostly we cook, although not all at the same time. I tried that once and it was a meltdown in the kitchen, not to mention the flour and sugar that got tracked from here to kingdom come. They are nearly always even-tempered, sweet, easy to be with, and great conversationalists, though for some odd reason, Temple has a Boston accent so I miss what she says sometimes. Cooking is our favorite thing to do. She told me I was the best cooker. I knew I loved that child.

November 2011

Old Skin

W E'RE ON THE COUCH watching Casper cartoons on my iPad and Temple says, "Have you noticed that I haven't pulled on your old skin today?" She has this thing about tweaking the skin on the back of my hand and watching it remain in a wrinkled peak.

I said, "Yes, I have noticed, and I appreciate it, thank you."

June 2012

Time-Outs

S ATCHEL NOW HAS A FOUR-YEAR-OLD SISTER.
Marching irately through my front door he says, "Oma,
you've got to do something about Temple. She gets
away with everything; she hits me, she doesn't listen, she's
completely out of control, and all they do is give her time-outs
and she doesn't even care."

"Why me?"

"Because you're the only one in the family who can do
anything about her!"

"So what do you have in mind?" I ask, knowing exactly
where this is heading.

"Well, could you spank her?"

"Oh sure. I smacked your bottom once and your parents
didn't talk to me for a month. I'm not laying a hand on that
child. Sorry, you're on your own on this one, Chickadee."

2012

A FICKLE
FOUR-YEAR-OLD

I STOPPED BY MY GRANDDAUGHTER'S pre-school to pick her up. She takes one look at me, and breaks into a wail, "I don't want to go with you! I don't like you!"

I say, "What happened? You liked me last week."

"I don't care," she sobs. "I don't like you anymore, and I don't want to go with you."

Packing her over my shoulder, I bundle her out to the car and strap her in her car seat. She's still wailing as we turn the car around to head to my house. I let her go on for another minute, then stop the car, turn around and level a look at her.

"Temple, knock it off. Now."

She looks at me, stops, and says, "Okay," like nothing ever happened. I've never seen a quicker turnaround in my life, not even on the stage.

2012

CHAR GIRL

I HAD MY FOUR-YEAR-OLD grandkidlet on Saturday. We're making cookies and she begs to take over mixing the flour.

"I do it, I do it. Let me, let me."

Cleaning up, as there was now batter everywhere, we put a load of towels in the washer.

She stops me again with, "I do it. I do it! Let me, let me!"

Then I pull out the vacuum to clean the floor dusted in flour.

Again, "I do it, I do! Let me, let me!"

While the cookies are cooling, Theda Bara looks up at me with her baby blues, puts the back of her hand on her sweet forehead and moans, "Work, work work! All I did today was work! I had to cook, I had to do laundry, I had to vacuum. I had to do everything! I'm exhausted!"

"Poor little char girl," I say in sympathy. "Here, have a cookie, it'll revive you."

2012

Hatfields
and McCoys

My ten-year-old grandson calls and says, hi Oma, it's me, Satchel, and I say hi Satchel, it's me, Oma. He asks if we are related to the Hatfields and McCoys. I say no, we're related to the Chatfields and Hoys. He says WHAT?!? I say, I can tell by your voice you're disappointed. Our family isn't nearly as interesting and I'm sorry, but the only connection is that they rhyme. They're from the South, we're from the North. He says, quite sadly, oh, right, okay, bye Oma. I say okay, bye Satchel.

I'm curious as to why he's watching *that* show on TV, on a school night, at that hour, not to mention that he attends a Waldorf school that frowns on television. I'll bet you dollars to donuts that his mother is not home.

May 2013

MURDERERS AND FORTUNE COOKIES

T HINKING IT WOULD BE FUN, Satchel and I took a day trip to San Francisco's Chinatown, Ghirardelli Square, and Pier 39. We made it there and back, but barely.

Going, we missed the Larkspur Ferry by ten minutes, so waited for the next one. Finally boarding, we sat on the windy upper outside deck so we could see the view. San Quentin and Alcatraz are fascinating to a ten-year-old boy who wants to know if you know anyone who got murdered and how it happened, and whether you actually know any real murderers, and who they killed. Luckily my Italian brother-in-law's brother was at one time in San Quentin for murder. We also have an ancestor, Valentine Hoy, who in 1898 was killed by Harry Tracy, the most infamous criminal of that day. My grandson was thrilled to hear the stories.

We made it to the City and were dropped of at the Ferry building. So far, so good. Then we found our way to Chinatown after asking a number of random strangers where to find the cable car. We grabbed an outside seat and hung on tight, hugging our legs close to prevent amputation from the passing cars, and actually got off on the right corner. I knew it because all the signs were in Chinese and the cable car driver winked at me, promising he'd tell us where to disembark.

The two of us wandered around Chinatown poking our heads in all the stores, ate dim sum at the Great Eastern Restaurant on Jackson, then bought a sack of dried mushrooms, some wonderfully weird fruit, and a bag of fortune cookies.

Gary Ruiz had suggested that while we were there, I see his Chinese doctor about my not-quite-healed kidney stone pain. We found the pharmacy just up the street. In the back room, the doctor tested my pulse, looked at my tongue, and wrote a prescription in Chinese characters for five bags of tea to the tune of $37. It was only $12 for the tongue and pulse advice; the translator told me the doctor said my back still hurts because there's sand in there from the stone, and the tea would cure me. Our arms loaded with fruit, dried mushrooms, fortune cookies and five bags of tea—we're talking five lunch bags, not tea bags—we head to Ghirardelli Square where the day starts to head downhill. We caught the bus going the opposite direction. We got off twenty minutes later when we figured it out, then waited a half-hour for the right bus to come along. As we boarded, we realized it was the same damn bus we'd gotten off a half hour earlier, with the same driver that I now wanted to seriously whack upside the head. We asked him the first time around if his bus would take us to the Square and he said yes, but failed to tell us not until he'd completed the route in the opposite direction. I put Satchel in charge of making the bus driver tell us exactly when and where to disembark. The driver does, but by this time I don't trust him. He knew that's where we wanted to go in the first place and didn't bother to point out to us that we couldn't get there from here.

He told us where to get off—which is *so* what I wanted to do to him. We thought we were lost again, as we were looking for a large brick building that is the entrance to Ghirardelli Square. We happened to be standing right in front of it. By this time, we were fading, so to sustain us, we headed for the Western cures of a lemon sorbet and a chocolate sundae. As I wasn't about to get on another wrong bus: we *walked* to Pier 39 where we finally found the magic store, then we *walked* back to the Ferry Building, hauling our substantial evidence of a Chinatown visit. We made the ferry by the hair of our chinny-chin-chins. We found places to sit on the lower inside deck: not only was it packed, it was now freezing out, so I sat with my head down and eyes closed for the half-hour ride. (I get seasick.) Then we *walked* the mile to the car. The lot was full in the morning when we got there, which is why we missed the ferry in the first place. In case you're not clear, Satchel and I are not what you'd refer to as "walkers."

Spent, we made it home to Sonoma by 7:30 to have dinner at Brooke's sister's house, which of course I couldn't find. I called my son, Matt—who was already there—confirmed we were in front of the right house, laid my phone on the trunk of a car in the driveway to put on my coat, then joined the party. Matt left the party at 9:00, got home, and called Brooke to tell her my phone is stuck on the trunk of his car. I got this sticky rectangle thing at a real estate conference; you peel off one side and attach to the back of your phone, and the other side is also sticky so when you leave it on the trunk of someone's car like some special kind of stupid, it holds it there and doesn't fall off and get run over by fifty cars while traveling a couple miles at 40 mph.

By ten I dropped into my bed, happy. I got my phone back. The dim sum was all that we hoped it would be. Chinatown was exotic, the fortune cookie factory was fascinating, though not terribly sanitary, and Satchel was fine that we didn't make it to the arcade. I'm not sure about the Chinese doctor—if in five days I'm still alive and the pain in my back is gone, I'll be overjoyed.

It will be a while before we take another trip. I have to tell you, five-year-old girls and the local park are much easier on me.

August 2013

Righteous Indignation

I PICKED UP MY GRANDDAUGHTER from school on her third day of kindergarten.

"So, how was it?"

"Well," she said, arms akimbo, "they have a lot of rules here."

"Like what?

"You can't throw rocks, you can't throw the bark, you can't peel the leaves off the trees, you can't climb the trees, and you can't jump off the merry-go-round when it's moving. You can't do anything here!"

"Could you do all that when in you were in pre-school?"

"Sure, you could do whatever you wanted in pre-school!"

"Ahh, I see. So how many kids are in your class?"

"Nine."

"That's a small class. How many boys and how many girls?"

"Seven boys and eight girls." I take note that she's inherited my mathematical skills.

If the remainder of the school year goes this way, I imagine she'll be spending a good part of her education in time-out. She can use the quiet time to work on her math.

September 2013

TUPPERWARE!

MY DILEMMA IS SOLVED: Tupperware! I saw a cartoon with two older women paying their respects to their friend lying in an open Tupperware casket, with the caption, "Edna would be so pleased... look–Tupperware!"

My grandson asked me if I wanted to be buried or cremated. I told him cremated because it's less expensive and makes a smaller footprint on the earth. Then I told him the REAL reason I don't want to be buried is because I don't want the bugs to eat me. He decided he'd be cremated too. I said he was a little premature in his planning, and I prefer that he go after me, but that I didn't imagine either one of us was proposing leaving anytime soon.

And now you're wondering why I'm having this conversation with a ten-year-old. Well, he asked.

October 2013

Food Fans

TEMPLE AND I COOK TOGETHER, then while we eat, we list all the ingredients in the dish.

During a dinner of Thai soup, she inquires, "What are you a fan of?"

Having no idea what she means, I say, "What?"

She says, "You know, food, what foods are you a fan of."

I say, "Oh, well, I'm a fan of shrimp, asparagus, sushi, and dark chocolate."

She then asks, "What are you not a fan of?"

I answer, "Black licorice, coffee, and wine."

So of course I ask her, "What are you a fan of?"

She says, "Broccoli and kale."

I say, "You are the oddest five-year-old I have ever met."

2013

ANGER ISSUES

SATCHEL ASKS, "Oma, do you know anyone with anger issues?"

I snort, "Do you mean besides nearly everyone in our family?"

Then we talk about Greek mythology and he tests me on all the gods and goddesses and thank Zeus, I remember. I can't remember where I left my keys or my purse, but I'm pretty darn good at recalling the underworld, Hermes, and Aphrodite.

January 2014

THE LIGHT OF DAY

WHEN I READ TO TEMPLE, or we watch movies, she sits close to me, slightly pinching the skin on the back of my hand or jiggling my underarm. I give her an evil look from slanted eyes and ask, "What are you doing?" She knows it drives me crazy.

"I can't help it," she sighs, "your skin is so wiggly. I like it."

She used to pull the neck crepe under my chin, which really drove me nuts. She doesn't do that anymore, which is one of the reasons she's made it to the age of six.

She had a sleepover this weekend. It was 100 degrees out and hotter inside, so I put on my purple shorts and green V-neck Sonoma tee shirt, tucked my hair behind my ears and joined her for a game of *Go Fish*. She's never seen me in shorts. Actually, it's been quite some time since anyone has seen me in a pair of shorts, including the light of day; my legs are so white you could read a book off their reflection.

She glances up and gushes, "Oma! You look REALLY cute!"

That's the nicest thing I could have heard, white legs and all, especially since Temple is quite the fashion plate, blessed with a sense of style from the get-go.

A couple years ago I was dressed for a dance; my blouse shimmered and my shiny silk skirt billowed as it caught the air when I came down the stairs. Her eyes widened and she gasped, "Oma! You look like a fairy princess! We could be fairy princesses together!"

Now how can you not adore someone that sweet, even if they have this thing about jiggling your wiggly skin.

July 2014

Princess Imelda

B IG SUR, CALIFORNIA. Camping is everything I remember, which is a lot of work, kind of grubby, and
not particularly comfortable. Other then Satchel having poison oak from stem to stern from his camping trip the
week before, and Princess Imelda having a meltdown because
she had to wear her tennis shoes instead of her sandals on the
hike, it was pretty easy... until she couldn't find her socks. My
teenage niece loaned her a pair.

"They don't match! One's pink and one's purple," she
wailed. "I CAN'T wear these."

"Temple, the bears don't care if your socks don't match.
They're SOCKS, we're in the woods, nobody cares."

"I care," she shoots back with a high-pitched caterwaul,
sobbing, "I want to wear my sandals."

After a few minutes of this, I tell her she has two choices.
"Don't go on the hike, or wear the tennis shoes and socks."

Even more tearful, and now prostrate in the dirt, she coun-
ters, "I don't like those two choices." I thought about a third
choice, but her parents have a thing about me beating their
children.

She went on the boulder hike, harrumphed the first half-
hour, did really well other than one scraped knee, and at the
end of the day grudgingly admitted it was good she wore the
tennis shoes and socks. However, she peeled them off the minute they got back to camp, dumping the socks disdainfully in
the dust outside our tent.

We left after dinner; between their schedule and mine, it was a one-night trip. Temple slept, Satchel read, I chewed gum and listened to Lyle Lovett and Lee Oskar on the drive home. When I realized my MapQuest directions were different from the nag in my dashboard, I surrendered and trusted the nag because it was dark out. We made it back to Sonoma in just under four hours, which was much better than the nearly six hours it took to get there.

My grandkids had a great time and want to go back, begging to stay longer next time. Of course they do. They're kids. They like sleeping on the ground. They think it's rollicking fun tipping like the *Titanic* trying to get dressed in a tent. They like bugs and burnt marshmallows. They don't care how bad they look in the pictures... unless the socks aren't a match made in heaven.

August 2014

THE BIRDS
AND THE BEES

SATCHEL SAYS, "Oma, you have to have a man and a woman to make a baby, right?"

I think, *"Why me, and why now?"* He can't ask me questions like this when we're alone? He wants to have a sex conversation with Miss Five-Year-Old Big-Ears sitting next to him in the back seat?

"Well, that was true at one time, but science has changed that some."

"How?"

"You need a sperm and an egg, but they no longer have to show up at the same time."

"How does that work?"

Thank goodness he only has time for one more question before we pull into their driveway. I go in and query his mother what Satchel knows about sex, as he's asking questions. She says his father discussed it with him. I wander down the hall and ask Matt if he's talked to Satchel.

My son looks at me in horror and says, "Eewwwww, no."

With a face palm, I slowly shake my head and leave.

2014

Go Fish

W E'RE PLAYING CARDS on my living room floor.
Boy child (age 11) has dealt.
Girl child (age 6) is waiting for instructions.
Boy child to girl child, "pick up your hand."

Girl child (in dead seriousness) lifts right hand and hovers it at arm's length, face down over the cards on the floor in front of her, as if she was at a séance.

Boy child rolls eyes, slaps himself on the forehead, and falls over backwards in disbelief.

"Why do I have to have her for a sister?"

I'm doing my best not to snort my brains out my nose because the girl child does NOT like to be laughed at. I pick up her cards, fan them, and tuck them in her hand for her.

We don't explain. It's better that way.

November 2014

Fashion Police

I WORE A SKIRT ON FRIDAY…
Girl fashionista, who wears her skirts slung low on her hips, "Is that a dress or a skirt?"

Me, "It's a skirt," and lift my sweater to show her.

Girl, in disbelief, "It's clear up to your WAIST?"

Boy grandkidlet to girl, "Oma can't help it… she's from Kentucky."

I'll bet those brats don't even know where Kentucky is.

November 2014

I Like Kids,
Preferably Fried

W HILE FIXING BREAKFAST TOGETHER, Temple says, "Oma, we should open a restaurant."

I tell her, "Sure, I'll be the prep cook because I'm the one who knows how to measure, and you be the one who pours and stirs and flips."

"I can only work two days a week during the summer," she says, "because I have swim lessons."

December 2014

STAND BY ME

THREE WEEKS AGO the boy child (age 11) stood by my side at my book-signing event at Readers', and read aloud a portion from *Passages from Behind These Doors*. The girl child (age 6) asked me beforehand if she could read some of it there, too.

I said, "Sure, just one problem."

She said, "What?"

"You don't know how to read."

She laughed and said, "Oh yeah, I forgot."

That changed last night. Side by side in my bed, propped up on pillows, she read her first words to me. Some words that make no sense, like 'when' and 'this,' and big ones too, like 'remember.' I helped some when she was stumped.

After ten minutes she lays her head back and says, "Whew, I'm sweating."

"I understand, it's hard work reading a whole book out loud for the first time."

When she finished the last page, she had a huge smile. When she closed the cover and carefully laid both her hands on it, I cried.

December 2014

WHITE SOCKS

THE KIDLETS WERE HERE for a sleepover. Last night the girl child was barefoot on the cold tile floor so I handed her a pair of socks.

With a look of disdain she says, "I'm SO not wearing those. They're scrunchy socks from the 80s! (This was the one who had the meltdown at the campground because her socks didn't match. Her brother borrowed the only white socks I had two weeks ago for basketball practice; he had new shoes, forgot his socks, and didn't want to get blisters. When doing the laundry, his mother asked him where the scrunchy 1980s cheerleading socks came from.)

I retort, "Oh you, who are SO wearing a tie-dyed shirt from the 60s?"

She informs me that tie-dye is back in.

Oh for godsakes... not only are my Swatch and high-waist skirts, like, so out of style, now apparently, so are my socks.

December 2014

TALK TO THE HAND

IT'S SATURDAY MORNING. As Temple unloads the silverware from the dishwasher she announces that the drawer is a bit of a mess. I offer to let her straighten it. She wants to know why I have five pairs of reading glasses in there. I tell her that's where they hide, which is why I have to buy new ones. She rolls her eyes. When she's done, I offer to have her straighten two more. She's appalled that they, too, are in such a jumble. After ten minutes she has them in great order. I had things in there that not only had I never used, but also wasn't sure what they were for. She proudly shows me both drawers, faces me and spreads her arms like guardian angel wings to protect them, admonishing me that I'm no longer allowed to go in either one, and if I do, they'd better look like this the next time she's here. I tell her to talk to the hand. Sheesh.

May 2015

FLIP OF A SWITCH

TEMPLE AND I ARE MAKING a mango smoothie. With the blender nearly full, I say, "You have to remember not to flip this switch up unless the lid is on."

She reaches over and flips it. In shock, we look at the walls and each other, now dripping in mango, banana, and yogurt.

"Like that?" she asks.

"Like that," I answer.

"Sorry," she says.

"I know," I say.

June 2015

POPCORN AND DIBS

THE GIRL KIDLET IS HERE for a sleepover and we are off to see *Inside Out* at our local theatre. It is $9.00 for me. I ask how much for a seven-year-old and Roger, the owner, says, "Also $9.00."

As we walk in the lobby, she tosses her blonde head and harrumphs, "Nine dollars for a seven-year-old? That's just plain mean."

I explain it's in 3D and we need to have special glasses.

Then she says, "We have to hurry because I want to sit in the front row."

We get our popcorn and Dibs and rush in to find one other person in the theatre. I told her I can't do the front row because I get motion sick so we share our food and she moves up to front and center when the movie starts. She doesn't like sitting next to me anyway because I jump and grab her when a scary part comes on; I scream the same way whether I'm about to be attacked by a great white shark or if a piece of seaweed touches my leg. No one who knows me sits next to me in a scary movie. And those who don't know me, soon move. She's been wise to that for years, so we usually sit separately.

After, I ask her what her favorite part was, and she says it was Joy dragging around Sadness by her foot. I tell her my favorite part was when Sadness realized how important she was in Riley's life.

Then she says, "I suppose you cried. You always do."

I did. As I had no Kleenex, I had to use the tiny crumpled napkin left over from our popcorn and Dibs.

After the movie we meander to the Tuesday night farmer's market for dinner and an hour at the playground, then we buy a cherry shaved ice and walk home under the nearly full moon.

July 2015

SOUS CHEF

WONDERFUL BIRTHDAY GIFTS are on my kitchen counter from Brooke, Matt, and the kids: a yogurt maker and Greek strainer, a small cookbook, fresh fruit, cinnamon, cardamom, vanilla: everything I need to make yogurt, except the cow.

I made my first batch. I thought it would be a no-brainer with only two ingredients, until I went over the three pages of directions six times, and read the dire threats of what can happen if not followed exactly.

After standing over the stove getting the milk to a certain temperature, though I suppose I need not stand over the stove the WHOLE time, and then cooling it to a certain temperature but not TOO cool, it looked easier than it was. For me, following cooking directions tosses me into the same depths of confusion and anxiety I sink to when I have to drive to the San Francisco Airport, terrified of missing a turn, ending up in Iowa. I become riddled with foreboding. I also know I tend to overthink anything that has to do with directions.

I figured it would be easier the second time; I started the yogurt at 11:00 in the morning, knowing I'd be up 10 hours later. That's how long it takes for milk to become yogurt if all goes as planned. However, I finished the process at 2:30, so now I have to stay up past midnight to turn the yogurt maker off and get the jars refrigerated.

The next week Temple was over, and we tried it together. Twenty minutes from start to finish. Ten hours later it was perfect. It so helps to have a sous chef.

September 2015

FOX TROT

SATCHEL HAD HIS FIRST DANCE LESSON THIS WEEK.
I said, "Okay, show me what you've got."

Facing one another in dance position, I put my left hand on his shoulder, his right arm around my waist, and my right hand in his left at face level.

He looks at me in shock, and as he backs away, says, "You're my grandmother!"

"Relax, Fred, we're not dating. We're in the kitchen, not at the prom. It's all good, and I know how to follow."

October 2015

GOODY GUMDROPS

EARLY MORNING CONVERSATION with seven-year-old girl child:
"Oma, you don't have any eyebrows."
"I know."
"What happened to them?"
"They're in my makeup bag and sprouting out my chin."
"Why don't you have them anymore?"
"As we get older, they thin out and turn gray."
"Nanny had eyebrows and she was in her 80s!"
"Well goody gumdrops for Nanny... "

October 2015

WHOO BOY

CONVERSATIONS WITH THE SEVEN-YEAR-OLD over the course of a morning:

Me: My wish for you when you are grown up is that you are kind, courageous, compassionate, and grateful. What do you want to be?
Granddaughter: Popular.
Me: Whoo boy...

Me: Do you think you'll play sports? (Her brother is athletic.)
Her: Nope.
Me: Not basketball? You're tall enough.
Her: Nope.
Me: Baseball?
Her: Nope.
Me: What about soccer? Or volleyball?
Her: Nope. Nope.
Me: Anything????
Her: Yep. I'm going to sing.
Me: Whoo boy...

Girl child: Is my dad handsome?
The Oma: Very.
The girl: Really?
The Oma: Yes, others comment all the time on how good-looking he is.

The girl: Hmmm. That's interesting. I always wondered what my mother saw in him.

The Oma: Whoo boy...

December 2015

Roots

DISTURBING THE DEAD, ANNOYING THE LIVING

W HAT CALLS US TO FIND THE ANCESTORS? It goes beyond a simple curiosity. We are taken over, compelled—as if possessed by something bigger than us that is begging to be revealed. There is one in almost every family called to be the scribe. I am but one of many in our clan's long line of storytellers. Like others, I'm called to gather and assemble the ancestors; to breathe life into them again as far back as we can reach. We take what we find and chronicle the facts of their existence, remembering their names, who they were, and what they did. We are the sum of who they were. Without them, we would not exist. We greet those who came before us, restoring their place in line. We scribe their stories and their histories. We search for them in public libraries, county records, and weed-filled or well-kept cemeteries. We comb through yellowed newspapers, family archives, lovely old letters, and photo albums. We find them! And in finding them, we find ourselves.

—Note: Inspired by "We Are the Chosen" written by Della M. Cumming, circa 1943

Taking a sidebar from finishing a family memoir, I spent five years working on family genealogy with my brother. Our research and records spanned from our ancestors' sailings to America to our parents' generation. We've done a commendable job of exploring our roots, bringing our ancestors together onto the same pages, compiling what would be a library shelf on the family lines. Gordon has been researching for years; I of late. But more important than the work we've done, is our time together doing it. As he is fourteen years older, I seldom saw him when I was growing up, so I'm grateful for this relationship we've created. We've visited Minnesota (our father's roots), and covered Wyoming, Montana, and Colorado (our mother's history.) We drove to Sonora where I was born, to Colusa where our parents met, to Brea where our mother is buried. We dug up information on our main ancestral lines, then put it all to rest, assembling and reuniting those no longer with us. I think it stems from my "keeping the family together" thing, and then some.

In the early morning and late at night I continue to research and add information to our lines. I make phone calls and send emails to unknown cousins. I search cemeteries. I track down pictures. Genealogy can be quite addictive, and being just a tad obsessive-compulsive, it keeps my fire fueled. I've created or contributed to nearly 7,000 pages of ancestors and related kin on Find A Grave, a kind of Facebook for the Dead, and have four websites in process on our Clemens, Chatfield, Hoy, and Chamberlin lines. Who'd have guessed that dead people would be my thing?

ALL ABOARD!

Dec 26, 1894 • Grand Junction, Mesa County, Colorado

CHARLES CHATFIELD MARRIED NELLIE CHAMBERLIN (they were my maternal grandparents) when he was twenty-three and she was twenty-one. Nellie—a nononsense Catholic girl who was exceedingly religious but had a mind of her own—refused to consummate their marriage. In frustration, Charles took his new bride for guidance to the priest who had married them. Father Carr sat Nellie down. He counseled her to go home and be a dutiful wife. Nine months later my grandmother gave birth to her first child, and over the next twenty years, delivered nine more.

1907 - 1913 • Sanders, Rosebud County, Montana

Around 1907 the family settled in Montana where Charles ran a large ranch near the hamlet of Sanders. Six years later, news came from family in California about the golden opportunities there: land was cheap, rice was the big new crop, and the weather was mild. Though Charles had become a highly successful rancher, Nellie was tired of the bitter cold. She persuaded Charles to sell their holdings and join the relatives. Her husband reluctantly went to town to finalize the deal. Four days went by with no sign of him, so Nellie sent a hired hand to look for him. When found, he was not only dead drunk, he'd gambled away all their money.

Nellie, fit to be tied, was still determined to move. She sold their only remaining property for $300: a wagon, and team of horses. In a rage, she readied her household for the long train ride west. She said nothing as she crated her New

Haven kitchen clock, a gift from Charles on the birth of their first child; nothing as she boxed her button collection, sewing needles, and nearly completed crazy quilt; nothing as she packed trunks with high-necked blouses, petticoats and bloomers. Tight-lipped, she packed her family pictures, black cast-iron pots, her righteousness and her past. With Nellie, wrath was silent.

While ironing her traveling clothes, in a continued fit of venom, she dropped the hot flatiron on her foot. The next day, with a fractured marriage and a broken foot, she would board the train in a wheelchair with her brood of nine. Nellie was forty years old.

When they heard, "All aboard!" they gathered their worldly possessions and filed on. Charles, her oldest at seventeen, carried his silver timepiece and his small leather-bound pocket diary. Leo, two years younger, carried his Case knife while her son Howard, a scrappy fourteen-year-old, carried a chip on his shoulder. Roy, not quite eleven, stayed close to Nellie, toted the food baskets and necessities for the little ones. Her first girl, Nella May, a wisp of a child not yet ten, had her hands full hanging onto four-year-old Verda and towheaded Arden, who was two-and-a-half. Gordon, seven-and-a-half and a dead ringer for a Chatfield, carried his mother's hatbox. Ina, only three months old and so tiny when she was born she slept in a shoebox, was in her mother's lap.

Three days behind his wife and children, Charles also arrived in California, hat in hand, hoping for forgiveness.

1913 - 1915 • Los Molinos, Tehama County, California

California was not the land of flowers that Nellie anticipated, but the weather was better. The family settled in Los Molinos; life was spare and my grandmother made do. Charles rice-farmed. Nellie raised the children. He puttered, tinkered, and gardened while she scrubbed floors, cooked stews, and mended shirts. He fed his chickens, she baked her bread, adjusting her recipe to the climate.

At the end of each week, he usually brought home little of what he'd made in the rice fields, his head hanging, his feet dragging—broke and drunk—so guilty she could smell his shame. Attempting to buy his way back into Nellie's good graces, he extended a peace offering to her—a gift wrapped in cloth. He wanted her to take it, to pardon him. She thought it was his earnings from his week's worth of work. It wasn't... it was an elegant tortoise shell comb for her long dark hair that she only let down at night.

"You fool!" she snapped. "We need food, not frivolity," and hurled the comb at his chest. "What you wasted on this could have fed us for a month!"

Nellie may have taken her wayward husband back, but she refused to forgive him. She also refused to share her bed, although she must have relented once, as their tenth child, my mother, was born two years later. They named her Noreen Ellen, but everyone called her Babe. Although Nellie wouldn't have taken a million bucks for any one of her children, she also wouldn't have paid a nickel for another, and Babe would be her last.

CRAZY QUILT

MY GRANDMOTHER STARTED her crazy quilt in 1895, the same year she started her family. Twenty years later, with the birth of my mother, Noreen Ellen "Babe" Chatfield, she completed them both.

During Nellie's first period of confinement (it was improper for pregnant and nursing women to be seen in public) her quilted piece grew. Her fine hands stitched rivers of gold, roads of onyx, and fences of pearl, connecting salvaged pieces of fabric—of little girls petticoats, Sunday-go-to-meetin' bests, Grandpa's fine vest, a bit of a wedding dress, a narrow strip of a cambric shawl. Patches of stripes and checks were stitched and cross-stitched with a jigsaw of shapes and hues. She saved her sewing scraps in a flour sack until she had a quiet moment to stitch the patchwork of smooth velvets, shiny taffetas, and bumpy poplins into a multicolored canvas for her embroidered birds, butterflies, and sweet honeybees that winged across her quilted legacy.

Over the years her bridle paths of alabaster threads gradually defined a landscape: a random patchwork of cattle ranches, rice fields and farmlands as if viewed through the keen eyes of a soaring red-tailed hawk. In her ankle-length skirts and her high-necked, long-sleeved blouses, Nellie rocked in her chair, her children in bed, her round sewing frame on her lap—silently laboring over her quilt, her only time of peace and solitude. By the gas lamp she stitched zig-zags of rainbow, dapples of color, and splashes of hope, creating a cover considerable enough to warm a generation of Chatfields.

As the family traveled by horse and buckboard through dust and storm, homesteading parts of Colorado, Wyoming, and Montana, the blanket, carefully folded and boxed, traveled with her. I can't imagine living through those times—through the harsh Rocky Mountain summers and winters, praying for better weather, for water and a good crop, for relief from the grasshoppers and the mosquitoes and the incessant biting of horse flies. Praying for her children down with whooping cough, croup, and ague—supplicating, kneeling, genuflecting... praying to God for everyone but herself.

I can't imagine having to haul water trying to keep things clean. Making one-pot meals in a black cast-iron kettle, the daily baking of buttermilk biscuits and apple cobblers and rough wheat breads, canning bushels of peaches and rows of corn to make it through another winter. Constant mouths to feed. Snow to shovel. Wood to chop. Animals dying, blizzards, buckboards, wagon trains, rattlesnakes, tornadoes, droughts—and babies—twenty years of birthing, nursing, rocking, changing, and bathing crying babies.

Maybe my grandmother's crazy quilt kept her sane. With the passage of time, like the passage of her family, its threads—winding and wandering through the generations—have worn, frayed, and unraveled. But like her family, its colors have withstood, endured, and upheld the tapestry of life.

Brilliantly.

ELEGY TO MY FATHER

Carl John Clemens (1905 – 1986)

ORN ON A MINNESOTA FARM, you milked cows, picked corn, and shocked wheat. You hated farming; that's why you left Minnesota, that, and your mother always telling you what to do. She cried when you left home. You were only sixteen. You had nine siblings, all with the same Clemens nose; your sisters looked like you in a wig. As a boy, you walked three miles to and from school in the snow—uphill—both ways.

Mom was 17 and you were 27, and a virgin, when you married. You were 43 when I, the youngest of your five children, was born. In Sonora you were a storeowner and town councilman: a big fish in a small sea. Things changed. Never speaking of Mom after she left, you forbid me to mention her also. You lost your business, your family, and your pride, paid your debts and left town.

You ate bottles of aspirin and rolls of Tums. When I was sick, you rubbed Vicks on my chest, gave me two Aspergums, and stroked my forehead. Sitting on the edge of my bed, you had tears in your eyes as you remembered the only time your mother comforted you was when you were sick. You taught me how to sew on a button, iron a shirt, and dust a banister. You let me put your donation envelope in the copper collection plate during Mass. You sang me German songs, found quarters behind my ears, and slapped your thigh at your own corny jokes. You gave me crisp two-dollar bills and a ballerina music box. We held hands when we went to Golden Gate

Park, Fleishhacker Zoo, and Fisherman's Wharf, my triple-time steps keeping up with your long stride. We took pictures with your Brownie. I have them still.

You were tall and upright, with wire-rimmed glasses, blue eyes and gray hair, and smelled of Old Spice, Vitalis, and Listerine. You wore a suit and vest, a tie, and your felt hat with two small red and black feathers in its brim. Your starched white shirt hid muscles you built from working in construction and delivering ice. Offering your arm, you walked on the curbside and tipped your hat. The first to stand and the last to sit, you also held chairs, doors, and umbrellas. You had no sense of direction—none—and missed the same turn-off three times. You tried to fix the living room door when it was sticking at the bottom. You sanded it, sanded it again, and sanded it some more. Then you sawed it. When done, it was an inch and a half too short at the top. You re-hung it anyway, and were embarrassed every time anyone mentioned the gap. You cooked double-thick lamb chops, canned green peas, and new potatoes, and you loved fresh crab, asparagus, and French bread. You read *Look, Reader's Digest*, and *The Saturday Evening Post*. Blood made you faint. Alcohol made you sick. Arrogance made you mad. The Ten Commandments, good judgment, and common sense directed your life.

You ran a five-and-dime on Haight Street. After work we drove home along Stow Lake, counting the rabbits and squirrels. When I got my learner's permit you let me drive, even though I scared you. When I was fifteen, you locked me out of the house while I was out with the neighborhood boys. When you told me to pack my bags, that I was going back to Carleen's, I cried. You let me stay. I worked with you every summer from the time I was twelve until I got married. You taught me to make change, stock shelves, and take inventory; to sweep the floor, run the register, and watch for shoplifters.

You taught me honesty and you taught me loyalty. You also taught me the cost of security: in twenty-five years of running a dime store, you never made more than $500 a month. You hated the Summer of Love, throwing buckets of cold mop water on the "goddam dirty hippies" when they slept against your shiny red-tiled storefront in the morning fog. You resented their freedom, sexuality and values, and detested their music, drugs, and panhandling. When the Haight—along with the world—changed, you closed the store.

On my wedding day you walked me down the aisle; you taught me to slow dance that day. You weren't fond of my husband, but you loved our babies. You cradled, tickled, and kissed them. You fed Matt his first watermelon and Jon his first ice cream. We played cards and cribbage and you taught my sons to play too. They were easy to beat and fun to cheat and you laughed when they caught you.

At the movies during the nude scene (it wasn't even a nude scene; she was standing at the second story window and slowly lifted her sweater off over her head while the cowboys watched from below), you were so startled you covered your eyes and threw your popcorn and Coke all over the people in the row behind us, your false teeth flipping out into your lap.

At your surprise seventy-fifth birthday party, you cried in the doorway of Sonoma's Depot Hotel. For your twenty-fifth wedding anniversary you had your tiny 1852 gold piece made into a pendant for Marie. You asked me to give it to her, knowing you wouldn't make it until then as cancer had spread to nearly every part of your body. You could no longer walk, eat, or turn over by yourself. When the black-robed priest quietly appeared at your bedside to give you the last rites, you blurted, "Oh shit," and ducked under the covers. Three days later, just before dawn, you took your last breath. They drove your body away in the back of an old brown station wagon.

We got to say goodbye. You got to say you're sorry. I got to say I love you.

I have your Kodak Brownie, pearl cufflinks, rosary beads, and your felt hat with the small red and black feathers. They all remind me of you, the best parts of you, and remind me of what I had.

Your daughter, *Catherine*

CRIPPLE CREEK TO SALT LAKE CITY AND BACK

M Y BROTHER, HIS WIFE MARIAN, and I just returned
from our fifth road trip of gathering family history:
searching through county records, newspaper archives, and historical museums, hunting for birth and death
records, local articles, pictures, deeds, wills and old maps—
things you have to go to actual locations to find. We make
Marian come as she has a sense of direction. On one trip to
Minnesota when she left us for five days to visit her sister,
Gordon and I changed hotels every day so we'd have our lug-
gage, as our chance of finding our hotel again was slim to
none.

My brother works on our family genealogy. I'm writing a
family memoir. I watch when they read the stories I pen. Marian laughs out loud or cries; she tells me she loves them.
Gordon looks like he's reading last month's weather report.

Gordon and Marian (they are in their early seventies) and I
(a generation younger), along with whomever in the family
we manage to entice to accompany us, pack what we need for
two or three weeks and set out to snoop wherever anyone will
let us. However, we have this uncanny knack for arriving at
the county museum, local library, or city hall on the day it is
not open, closed for remodeling, or just as they are locking up
for the night.

In the past four years we have explored the Sacramento
Valley, the gold country of Northern California, the cemeteries of Southern California, five western states, and our

father's family farm in Minnesota—visiting cousins and taking pictures of homesteads and headstones. Our latest road
trip covered 5,000 miles on a 4,500-mile foray. We drove
through Nevada, a small corner of Arizona, the Rockies of
Colorado, the expanse of Wyoming and the flatlands of Montana. The extra 500 miles we spent heading off into the wild
blue yonder. Gordon won't look at map so he makes Marian,
but when she tells him which way to go he doesn't believe
her. I can't read a map and get carsick if I take my eyes off the
horizon, so I stay out of it.

My brother always tries to convince me to eat at Subway.
Forget it. I drag them to ethnic or organic restaurants. At dinner I order water with no ice, a salad with no onions, a veggie
burger with no mustard, and could they please leave the dress-
ing on the side.

Gordon leans into me and asks, "Can't you just order
something like it comes on the menu? You are like dining
with Sally in *When Harry Met Sally*," and I snicker, "that's
not the scene that comes to *my* mind in that movie... "

In Nevada, our Hoy cousins graciously put us up for a
night. I want to live in their house; their linens cost more than
my furniture, not to mention Celine Dion lives in the neighborhood. They fix us a fabulous meal—another reason I could
move in with them. My brother comes in the living room and
looms over me as I sit on the couch admiring a very good
copy of a Rembrandt. "How do you want your steak cooked?"
I don't eat meat but note the look on his face and have the
common sense to say, "medium rare." He says, "right answer." And just between you and me—it was delicious! Our
mutual ancestors were in the cattle business, and for my
cousin's birthday, his wife had given him a miniature HOY
branding iron. The two-inch letters burned into the steaks

were a nice touch, as was the homemade strawberry ice cream.

Marian always makes us two-dozen Toll House cookies. Every trip I eat my half and half of Gordon's half. She eats almonds and prunes. Yakking away from too much sugar and chocolate, a hell or a damn falls out of my mouth and my brother tells me to quit my swearing. Again. I try really hard not to swear around him, but I forget. Into the second week he says do you HAVE to swear ALL the time? I inform him that puke is not a swear word and that swearing MAYBE once a day is not ALL the time and that I'll make him a deal: if he uses his turn-signal, I'll quit swearing. My brother is unaware that turn signals are standard equipment on cars, and have been for years. He has this thing where he can't decide if he's turning left. The oncoming traffic also has no idea what he might be planning. He hesitates until they get close. Then he whips right out in front of them. I have this thing where I slide down my seat, throw my feet up to block the airbag, close my eyes, cross my heart and mutter, "Oh sweet Jesus."

He says, "I didn't know you were religious."

I say, "Only when you're driving."

Of course I won't mention the day in downtown Denver when *I* turn right onto a one-way street in rush hour and have to back up their shiny new SUV away from a stream of screeching, honking traffic. I'd also rather not talk about the next day when I turn left off a one-way street into the left lane and drive a whole block on what is not a one-way street, not able to figure out what the hell the guy coming at me thinks he is doing. Marian, who is trying to read a Denver map so big that it blocks half the steering wheel and hangs two feet out the passenger window glances up and casually suggests I might want to pull over a couple of lanes. Thankfully, Gordon isn't in the car either time. He fails to see the humor in moments like these. Having played the sousaphone in high school and college, he's in horn heaven at a four-day Tuba and Euphonium Conference (which is part of the reason we took this trip), hanging out with 500 tuba players, most of whom I notice have the same body shape as the brass instrument they play. But I must say, 500 tubas a-tuba-ing is a magnificent sound. The three evening concerts we attended were wonderful.

We drive through Bryce National Park where wind, water, and magic have cut the limestone into a landscape of bizarre shapes of mazes, slot canyons, and elegant spires of hoodoos. We are equally stunned by Zion National Park where the red and pink sandstone cliffs look like sandcastles built in desert canyons, their massive walls soaring to a vast blue sky. Rocky Mountain National Park also takes our breath away, and not just because of the altitude. We spend the afternoon at Custer's last stand. Heart-wrenching—not for Custer (that's my opinion, not my brother's), but for what this country did to its Native Americans.

At the Denver History Library we are ecstatic with each new discovery, whooping and high-fiving, clapping one another on the back. The librarian continually pokes her head into the room with a sharp look. Gordon and I sit side-by-side, hunched over giant microfilm machines, rolling through reel after reel of old newspapers, me going half-blind from the bad print and queasy from the movement. I get clammy, stagger to the ladies' room to throw up, then I wander over to the local history section to look up things in books where the pages don't move. Marian comes back from being buried in the archives all morning, thrilled with the great find in hand and presents it to her husband. Gordon barely glances up, telling her he already has that record. She disappears for several hours. He finally notices she's missing and asks where she is and I say she's at the courthouse looking up records for HER family, and filing for divorce. He hadn't seen the look on her face.

Marian and I spend much time together in ladies restrooms laughing so hard we cry and slide to the floor while Gordon is in the hall, waiting stiffly against the opposite wall with tight lips and crossed arms. She gets a medal for spending hours poring over microfilm and old newspapers searching for snippets about our Hoy, Chatfield, and Chamberlin lines. You couldn't pay me to spend that much time looking for information about someone else's family, even if I was married to them. Perhaps that's another reason I'm not married.

After Colorado we don't make it to Nebraska. Instead, we decide to head for Montana as my brother thinks Montana is on the way home. Marian rolls her eyes. She's been married to him for fifty years. I'm somewhat suspicious about the whereabouts of Montana, but think it a fine idea, as I too want to find the ranch our grandfather gambled away. After Montana, we head for Utah.

The only disappointment of our three weeks: after having driven for sixteen days in the car, the Mormon Family History Library in Salt Lake City was closed on Sundays, the only day we had to spend there. Of course.

"WHAT? We've driven almost 4,000 miles to come to THIS library and you are closing in THREE HOURS and won't be open TOMORROW? WAAAH! How can that BE?

"Tomorrow is Sunday," the greeter says kindly. "The library is not open on Sundays."

"Why not?" I ask.

"For religious reasons."

"Religious reasons? What does that have to do with anything? You're not Catholic!"

Marian and Gordon have wheeled away from me. Dejected, I try not to cry as I join them in the elevator. They pretend they don't know me. But we still discover a fair amount in those three hours.

The next morning (since the damn library is closed) we set out for the Mormon Tabernacle Choir, which I have wanted to hear forever. During the hour-long rehearsal the usher standing five feet from me has to natter brightly, "watch your step, watch your step" through the WHOLE performance. Like the lights aren't on? Like everyone is blind? Like 200 people haven't already walked down 50 steps to get to her landing and not one has tripped and needed to be rushed by ambulance to the hospital? I was aggravated enough that she yapped through the entire concert, but when she pulled out a piece of cellophane wrapped candy—oh my God—the woman is lucky she's still alive. I was close to caning her. But it didn't get ugly until we left. The three of us actually make it back up all those stairs without falling. When we reach the lobby, one of the white-haired ushers observes me foaming and twitching and has the temerity to ask me how the concert was. I latch onto his gray lapel and get so close our noses nearly touch.

"How was the concert? You want to know how was the concert? RUINED, that's how the concert was! RUINED!"

Out of the corner of my eye I see that Marian and Gordon have peeled away, acting like they have never ever seen me before in their entire life. As I wind down my rant regarding cellophane wrappers and lack of usher training, I notice how wide this man's eyes are. Taking a deep breath I slowly unpeel my fingers from his lapel and pat it gently back down and thank him for inquiring, murmuring, "I feel much better now, much better. Thank you." My brother and sister-in-law have scattered like ants disturbed at a picnic.

We come home a day early, bleary and stiff from hours of driving, every empty space in their no-longer-new hybrid littered with crumbs and stuffed with stacks of information, wishing we'd had more of Marian's cookies, happy. Was our trip a success? You betcha! Did we find everything we were looking for? No, but enough to satisfy us until the next journey. We found pictures we didn't know existed, nearly a hundred newspaper articles that filled in a lot of blank holes, and a number of books others had written about the family. However, we also discovered that the best family legends we had in the books we're putting together aren't even true!

Grandpa didn't gamble away the ranch. They never owned a ranch. And if they had owned a ranch, it wouldn't have been worth $150,000. Hell, in 1915, you could have bought the whole godforsaken state of Montana for $150,000. They were giving the land away to homesteaders. Why would anyone pay for it?

And not only was James "J.S." Hoy, my great-grandmother's brother, not castrated for sleeping with a med student's wife (turns out he had mumps as a baby), Henrietta Wilcox didn't poison him either.

Truth: the downside of research. The most interesting legends turn out to be just that. Legends. I suppose that's why I titled our family history *Lore, Libel and Lies*—so I could leave them in.

July 2006

BLOODLINES

Though I knew not the uncles who slept in gold dust,
I've been told whom they hated
and whom they could trust.
I read which ones fiddled, who sang and who danced;
I hear they worked hard—wonder if they romanced.
I've met not the aunts, the women of kind,
but can guess of their hopes and where they were blind.
Am told how my grandfathers laid down their life,
I know where they lived and who was their wife.
I know what they died of: bad kidneys and rage,
some died of weak hearts, others died of old age.
Some died from smoking, from whiskey, from sin;
others from cancer, and a few did themselves in.

Those departed before us, their stories are gone,
'til they came on the *Diligent* and on the *St. John*.
They arrived as stonemasons, blacksmiths, and deacons,
planting the New World as seekers and beacons.
Peter left Consdorf and sailed 'cross the sea,
laid roots in Mazeppa—my father's history.
George hailed from Sussex to start a new life
and settled in Guilford with children and wife.
Was Henry the smithy? Or did he make shoes?
Ask dear Grace or David, they gave us the clues.
Though futures are clouded by sins of the past—
history's rewritten by those who come last.

I'll make note of those briefly from whence I did come:
the Leinens and Tomlinsons and Reilands are some;
the Snavelys, the Smiths, the Shades I give due,
the Sumners and Surdams, must mention them too.
But where are the Masticks, a family of yore?
And what of the Andersons, a part of my core?
The Chamberlins—well-preserved by others held dear,
but the Harringtons—a mystery,
the Vonadas—not here.
I descend from the Clemens, the Nigons, and Hoys,
though most familiar with Chatfields
—their mistakes and annoys.
The stories I've heard were not always true,
passed down through the family and now onto you.

Regarding our women so little was written,
so little recorded 'bout how they were smitten.
These mothers of mothers and mothers of mine
were grown from seed you don't always find.
Herein lie their legends, their letters and lore
with tintypes and photos that show what they wore.
I know what they cooked and what they were taught,
I know some were Catholic—which tells me a lot.
They were strong and defiant—ruled by what's right,
married men that some left, making do with their plight.
I presume who they were by looking at me,
our blossoms and thorns
twining through this same tree.

Through bloodlines, through love,
through bad luck or tether—
it matters so little what binds us together.
We're scattered and distant all over the place
but still all related by marriage or grace.
Those gone before are a part of me still,
a dram of my blood, a slice of my will.
They watch over me with wonder and trust,
to guide me from birth till I too turn to dust.
I've sat on their headstones—these relations of past
and pondered and wondered how I am like cast.
I sense all their voices, they touch me in dreams,
I glimpse at their lives to unearth what mine means.

LORD LOVE A DUCK

There once were three brothers, from England did flee
Sailed on the *St. John* in good company.
Our line comes off George, ten progeny past,
Begetting the Chatfields of which I am cast.
They're an interesting bunch, left their mark in the world
With a wide path to follow, a history unfurled.

Why bother to gather this family so long?
"What does it matter? They're all dead and gone!"
To answer that question I gave it some thought...
"It matters to me," and then I was caught.
Some tasks are for money, this one was for love,
And I often seemed guided by invisible glove.

This clan fills my dreams, drops me clues here and there;
I pay close attention; seek out others who care.
Dead ends we do reach: "Where oh where is this kin?
Relax. They'll show up! They all want to be in!"
So off on the hunt, searching records and such
We piece it together with finishing touch.

We find bibles and wills and records of war,
We find letters and pictures and essays and lore.
Herein are the brothers, the sisters and aunts
The fathers and mothers—their stories and haunts.
They built railroads and ranches, grew potatoes and rice,
Left a heritage rich with their work and advice.

The trail heats with Isaac some hundred years back,
He—father of Grandpa, the black sheep of this pack.
Isaac lost his son Wirt. Dell's death caused great sorrow.
Clark buried Louisa but soon married Miss Morrow.
Next we have Ida, with no trace, disappeared...
Found drowned in the river, as her family had feared.

My favorite was Ora, a girl of sixteen—
Eloped with her cousin—caught betwixt and between.
Her beloved was Clara, ten springs older than she,
Made headlines in Denver with a tad too much glee.
Then along came Ray Sawyer, played the organ in Reno,
Wrote a book about gamblers, dice, blackjack and Keno.

His arrest hit the papers for dabbling in crime
Though we failed to find out if he ever did time.
"Lord love a duck!" Cousin Aura did write
When I sent her the news of Miss Ora's plight
Along with Ray's photo and news clipping besmirched,
"Good gracious!" she piped, "what a scandalous search!"

The spouses and children, I've taken a look
And determined they all should live on in this book.
For if not for their presence we wouldn't be here
With the grant of their legacy to hold very dear.
Droopy eyelids, bad kidneys—yes, those we did get—
Along with not speaking to half of our set.

They all made a difference, these men and the wives
To better their country, their families and lives.
Their spirits survive in our hearts and our hands,
Gifts of courage, of music, of their love of the land.
Strong women, good men—these Chatfields can toast,
Tis an honor and privilege to be part of this host!

January 2007

EMILY AND THOSE HOY BOYS

As rivers cut canyons through Rockies to bays
the Hoys traveled westward in pioneer days.
They fought for the Union,
Frank, wounded in battle,
then homesteaded Brown's Hole
where they branded their cattle.
They were ranchers and farmers and
bull-whackers of yore,
horse breeders, schoolteachers, and miners of ore.
They were writers and poets, a politic few,
they were German and English, a Swiss woman too.

Herein are their timelines, their letters and lore,
with charts of ancestors and children they bore.
Newspaper clippings, records, and wills,
excerpts and photos and warranty bills.
They all tell this history so much better than I,
this trail left behind from those now all gone by.
I penned stories of kin my brother explored,
he combed through the records—such tasks I deplore.
Names, facts, and figures, they interest me some,
but tis the echoes of tales that I yearn to plumb.

The Hoys sued each other, Grandpa gambled the ranch
(he, a fool with the whiskey—
an ache through our branch).
Davis cheated on Emily and cared not the least,
Ada's vows to Doc Chambers were
undone by the priest.
J.S. while in France was castrated with knife,
caught in the act with a med student's wife!
James perished from poison! Tracy shot Val and ran!
Harry fasted five weeks—up and died from that plan.
The query that actually started this game
was, "What's the 'S.' stand for in Emily's name?"

Some mysteries still linger, some relations not found,
like what caused Frank's death and
where laid in the ground?
What happened to Winnie? From what did she perish?
A tintype of her I truly would cherish!
A.A. had three daughters—what happened to them?
And what of wife Frances—his crème de le crème?
There's no trace of Lizzie, in shadow she's sunk...
disappeared like Minerva and J.S.' trunk!

Missing records and pictures and letters of yore
keep me digging and searching—I know there are more!
One more trip, one more hunt, another call I will make
just to find out for clarity's sake.
But does it matter if I know not all that occurred?
No, though at the end of the day you may rest assured
that I'll let out a whoop and drop down on my knees
if I ever discover the answers to these!

TOSS OF
THE COSMIC DICE

WHY BOTHER? I MEAN REALLY? They're dead. Who cares about the past, and what difference does it make? But here's the deal: sometimes we do something for its own sake, or sometimes simply because we want to.

There was a five-year period between finishing my family memoir and getting twenty short stories from it published. In that five years, I worked on my genealogy, gathering all the historical facts, figures, and tales I could glean about my parents and their lines. I didn't plan on dancing with the dead any more than I planned on having teenagers or going into real estate. Sometimes things just happen.

From adding flesh to the bones of our ancestors and breathing life into them as far back as I could reach, I came away with a sense of my genetic make-up. When I started this, I knew little beyond my grandparents' names. Then I came across a picture of my Grandma Nellie with her sisters. How could I not know that she had sisters? I nearly fell over, partly from realizing how clueless I was.

That's what started me on the hunt. I spent untold hours on the computer (you have no idea) and tracked down other relations, all the while gathering pictures, records and letters. I now know my history and my heritage. I have a lot of the same traits and tendencies that those who came before me did. I gained insight about my culture. I came away with a love of history. I hadn't remembered squat about those who settled this country, about planters and pilgrims, about the Revolutionary and Civil Wars, or WWI and WWII. Did I sleep through high school history? I know I had the book as I carried that weight back and forth to school every day. Apparently I'd not opened it. My ancestors were part of all that, and somehow I'd missed it.

Actually, I find it stunning that I'm here at all. Truly, what are the odds? A toss of the cosmic dice? First of all, each of those who came before me had to meet, then live long enough to procreate, then their children had to repeat that process. There is a long line who've been part of this country for generations, all of whom contributed to my very being. I stand on their shoulders, for if not for them, I would not be here.

Those of us who work on our family lines have an obsessive dedication and curiosity that surprises even us. It's remembering that's important, offering an understanding of our imprint as a member of our culture and family, and who we are as human beings. Knowing where I came from reveals to me who I am. I'm blessed to be one of the keepers of the lines, alongside my brother—who has been at it for years—along with a number of both near and distant cousins. It's given me a relationship with them, among untold others, who've also contributed what family information they possessed. Many with whom I connected were in their 80s and 90s; they were thrilled to talk to someone who was interested in their lives, and generously shared their stories and pictures with me. They were also grateful to have a remembering of their past, and I'm thankful that they were able to share it with me before some of them died.

Not everyone is fascinated by genealogy, particularly someone else's. I've been to events where speakers rhapsodized at length about their kith and kin; it was painful. It was also an "aha" moment. I realized that we do all this work, and really, nobody else gives a popcorn kernel! I discovered nothing bores me more than listening to the droning of another's line, yet oddly enough, there's nothing I like better than the puzzle of sorting out my own. I love the quest, and the satisfaction of having missing pieces fall into place.

Gathering my kin also fulfills a need in me; it's part of my wanting to keep the family together. I do it for my ancestors; I do it for my family still living, and for those yet to come. I do it because it's important to me. That's why I bother.

LINEAGES

I am.
I am from
Leinen and Nigon,
from Chamberlin and Hoy.
I am from Clemens and Chatfield,
from Surdam, Sumner, Smith, Shade, Mastick, and Tomlinson
too. From Matthew, Isaac, Finley, and Charles.
From Barbara, Eliza, Emily, and Nellie.
I am from soldiers who fought for the Union and from a nurse
who tended them. From singers, shopkeepers and teachers,
from miners, writers, and preachers. From wagon trains and
railroads. From hard work and harder lives. I am from cattle
ranches and farmlands, from sowing and plowing and reaping.
From whiskey and ale, from betting and bad odds—
and from the fallout of it all.
I am from Noreen and Carl, who were like sin and prayer.
What ever in the world made those
two think they could stay together?
I am from dime stores and small towns. I am from sweet peas,
green peas, and green tea. I am from one-pot meals.
From white beans, white bread, and white rice.
I am from holy water and rosaries, from *Hail Mary* and *Our
Father*, from mea culpa. I am from *Little Women* and *Nancy
Drew*, from *I'm a Little Teapot* and *The Hokey Pokey.* From
pop-beads, pee-wees, paper dolls, pick-up-stix, skate keys,
comic books, and jacks. From coin collections and stamp
collections and collections of cobalt blue glass bottles.
I am from bad kidneys, bad eyes, and bad blood.

I am also from a long line of sharp-tongued women.
From list makers, rule makers, and rule breakers—from
umbrage and resentment. From complaining, carping, and
keeping score. From they don't speak, we don't speak.
Sometimes it seems impossible to do it differently, to break
this invidious pattern of ours.
And sometimes it is easier not to even try. I am from good
intentions and unattended sorrows. From courage and hope
and grace. I am from extended arms, extended kindness, and
extended family. I am grateful.
I am from a company of strangers,
this family, of it, but not in it,
watching from the sidelines, taking notes, sifting through
our story and writing down our history, wondering
what directs us, what pokes us and prods us
and has us be who we are, questioning
how I fit into the whole catastrophe,
and, at the end of the day—
knowing I belong.
I am they.
I am me.
I am.

About Catherine Sevenau

"Neurotic?" Catherine wondered. "I may be on the obsessive compulsive side, but I've never thought of myself as neurotic!" However, with the circumstances around her childhood, she should be.

Sevenau weaves her insightful collection of spunky vignettes together like a fine cloth threaded with hurt, love, death, and laughter. The universal themes of redemption and coming home will strike a nerve; her story of good intentions and unattended sorrows will touch your heart.

Her stories are tales worth telling, poking fun at the human condition, her family, and herself. In this brave uncovering to find her place in the family and comprehend her unhinged mother, Sevenau discovered herself instead. Looking back with clarity and perspective, she embraced the events of her growing up and came to understand that what transpired were gifts in disguise; that all the complexities in her life happened *for* her and not *to* her.

Catherine Sevenau is an avid swing dancer, real estate maven, irreverent humorist, and author, depending on the hour. These stories from her blog and beyond comprise her second book.

Also by Catherine Sevenau

Passages from Behind These Doors
A Family Memoir

Chatfield Historical Website
www.ChatfieldHeritage.com

Ancestral Family Lines
Google: Find a Grave Catherine Sevenau

©National Portrait Gallery, London

Queen Elizabeth I
by Unknown English artist
oil on panel, circa 1600
50 1/8 in. x 39 1/4 in. (1273 mm x 997 mm)
NPG 5175
www.npg.org.uk/collections/search/portraitLarge/mw02070/
Queen-Elizabeth-I

The digital artist Sarah Niebank created the image of the Queen Bee on the cover of this book. The use of the picture of Queen Elizabeth was with the permission from the National Portrait Gallery in London, England.